Media in the Midst of War

The Gulf War from Cairo to the Global Village

This edition published in 1992 by
The Adham Center Press
113 Sharia Kasr el Aini
Cairo, Egypt

Dar el Kutub No. 8388/92
ISBN: 977-00-3966-7

Printed in Egypt by Technotex Graphic Arts, Alexandria

CONTENTS

Preface

The invasion of Kuwait focused the world's attention on a media event -- the Gulf war. Coverage of the conflagration stimulated an extraordinary amount of analysis of the circumstances behind the TV screen, radio speaker, and printed page. At the time of this writing the diversity of media research and analysis was extensive. Professional and academic associations have sponsored studies, conferences have presented individual research endeavors and books have been published, with others in press. However, the thrust of research has so far been targeted from a Western media perspective.

The approach of this volume offers insights to the outputs of media at the core of the Arab world -- Egypt. Studying sources and coverage originating in Egypt lets us explore media in the midst of war. While the contents are principally related to Egyptian broadcast and print journalism, America's CNN and the British Broadcasting Corporation's Arabic World Service have been included as they were also key players in Gulf crisis and war reporting from the Gulf.

The effort which unfolds below explores newspaper and electronic journalism with a multifaceted approach. Sections of the volume give perspectives on the development of Egyptian media to afford a clearer understanding of why coverage was uniquely Egyptian and not simply a mirror of the Western media. Other pieces detail the styles and goals of those Western media that covered the crisis and war from Egypt. There is a combination of quantitative and qualitative styles as contributors pursue their venues. The literature references and appendices can provide those interested in exploration of development communication, Gulf crisis media and case study data with current resources. Let me stress that this work has not been an attempt to do political or sociological interpretation of Egyptian media content. Nor is it intended as a compendium of all Egyptian media, as, for example, no magazine analysis or discussion has been included.

The first unit of this work focuses on the broadcast media of radio and television. Following introductory comments on war journalism, I discuss

CNN's introduction to the Egyptian public. As a re-broadcast, in English, it made media hype rather than an impact. The development of independent Arab satellite media and its use during the crisis is reviewed in Hussein Amin's contribution on Egyptian SpaceNet. SpaceNet's role in information dissemination to a primarily Arab-Egyptian audience is detailed. Magda Bagnied presents the administrative and programming responses of ERTU radio and television operations management during its crisis coverage.

The second unit examines Egyptian newspapers' approach to the Gulf crisis, the war, and its aftermath. Egypt's press has had a longstanding interest in Iraqi events. Dina Lamey's essay on pre-invasion and post-invasion Egyptian press coverage of Iraq empirically states common sense: friends get positive coverage; enemies don't. James Napoli's analysis of press coverage during the crisis follows. Taking a development communication perspective, Napoli examines Egyptian editorial policy toward the Gulf crisis and adds to this a 6-week analysis "window" of Egyptian press coverage. Sonia Dabbous reviews Egyptian press laws, then presents results of her front page content analysis of representative government and opposition papers. Political caricature can be as incisive as editorial writing and Richard Boylan's description of Egyptian newspaper cartoons establishes this point. The samples represent some Egyptian public "mindsets" during the Gulf crisis. As a complement to the cartoon visual imagery, Hussein Amin analyzes the use of press photojournalism in government and opposition newspapers.

I have included a main unit whose focus is not Egyptian media. What the Gulf crisis and war should have made abundantly clear is that global media is the operationalized concept. As CNN and BBC worked from "within," they may have unknowingly impacted Egyptian media -- for better or for worse. Ted Turner, speaking at Montana State University's symposium on "Media and Social Responsibilities," reviewed CNN's foundational news policies in relation to the Gulf crisis. CNN became the most identifiable medium for the confrontation, and naturally, the ensuing kudos and condemnations. His personal perspective on CNN's philosophy is juxtaposed with internal documents to provide insight to CNN's legal and ethical policy determinations in war coverage. Though not a journalist, he spoke firmly to advocate press access in concert with governmental restrictions on the media. The BBC World Service Arabic broadcasts achieved enhanced program credibility during the crisis and war. John Tusa explains the goals, methods and results of BBC efforts. It may be likely that "BBC lessons learned" have direct relevance for global media, let alone those that worked "in the belly of the beast." Considering implications of media coverage of the crisis and war as the unveiling of "New World Order" Global Village communications, S.A. Schleifer's essay based on his Gulf reporting experiences concludes the unit. His point that the Western media and mind and Arab information ministries have not understood the coverage "failure," certainly is a unique position. One might ponder the long-term impact of this media manipulation: Has there been victory or failure of politics or media, or both?

Our intent has been to provide an exploration of coverage of the Gulf crisis in the hope of contributing to an understanding of these events and issues from Arab media orientations and frames of reference. Given the frequent accolades and/or criticisms of Western coverage of the crisis, we believe this volume should, at the least, clarify "Arab-Egyptian" media responses during the Gulf crisis. We hope readers will also appreciate the head-to-head presentation of the Egyptian press, ERTU, the BBC, and CNN.

If the comprehensiveness of this volume is to stress any overall focus, it may come from the position that journalists and the media they represent must pass beyond territoriality and vested nationalistic interests. Other topic-specific academics also make this point. Liebes (1992), in concluding an analysis of U.S. and Israeli *intifadeh* and Gulf war television coverage, said:

> It is not surprising, therefore, to discover that journalists' treatment of their own country's wars is different from the way they handle other people's wars. The 'surprise,' if any, lies, rather, in observing how reluctant journalists are to acknowledge this dilemma.... Perhaps a more honest response would be to acknowledge that the luxury of the detachment offered by the ideology of 'objectivity,' 'neutrality,' and 'balance' is reserved for reporting other people's troubles, rather than one's own (54).

I am appreciative of the efforts displayed by my colleagues to develop their research for this volume. Dan Tschirgi and Nicholas Hopkins provided valuable and constructive comments on early drafts and I give them a hearty thank you. Special thanks go to Nevine Khalil, as she assumed the responsibilities of serving as the work's administrative assistant.

Finally, decisions regarding material inclusion, sequencing, editing, and overall point-of-view are the responsibility of the editor. Shortcomings on such points are my responsibility.

Ray E. Weisenborn
November 1992
Cairo, Egypt.

Egyptian Media: Radio and Television

Cool Media, The Gulf War and Then -- CNN

Ray Weisenborn

Although war is the epitome of human weakness, it has historically been an aberrant form of social entertainment. During the American Civil War there were excursions by the social elite to battlefields to witness the day's events. Unwarranted anticipation of Napoleon's victory at Waterloo led the carriage class to witness the clash while holding picnics. For centuries, armies travelled with a social support cortege and chronicles were sent home to tell of victories or defeats. The chroniclers have stood with Alexander and Pershing, Montgomery and MacArthur. Often the attempt to witness an event for history has resulted in the image presentation of pure ego. When MacArthur returned to the Philippines as promised, the event was photographed several times until the "right" shot was made of the General wading ashore. And so the media continue to report the failure of mankind to settle differences amicably.

The introduction of electronic journalism to the battlefield, as in the "television war" from Viet Nam, significantly affected journalistic processes. Time and distance, as experienced by Matthew Brady during the American Civil War and Ernie Pyle in World War II, have vanished as the public has become participants; the audience does not want to view events retrospectively.

Coverage of war has in many respects erased the boundaries of differing attitudes, nationalistic perspectives, and the successes or failures of belligerent actors. Media coverage is technologically dependent and success is, in large part, determined by those who control what Alvin Toeffler called the infospheres of the world. Concern with the implications of those spheres has been constant for more than two decades in analyses comparing the value of free and balanced information flow with various factors promoting media dependency.

A frequent cry from Third World countries is they are being maligned, manipulated and misrepresented by the Western-dominated media system. Standard reference is made to American media incursion. Arguments of cultural imperialism, economic Machiavellianism, and political pressuring are frequently made by Third World journalists. UNESCO reports define the problem from a "rich" North and a "poor" South perspective. Egypt is no exception, and the Gulf crisis media from the locus of events was predominantly Western media coverage (Revzin, 1990; LaMay, 1991, El-Desoukry, 1992).

But on the micro level, the Egyptian media are a little surprising. Egyptian television's bootlegging of international satellite feeds is common. *The Egyptian Gazette* often lifts photographs and stories from *Time*, *Newsweek*, and the *International Herald Tribune* -- and usually omits all credits. For example, the March 3, 1992, *Gazette* contained photographs and stories from the current *Time* issue with individual and wire service identification left out. While this point may beg the question of "fair or foul ball" being called for media dependence, Egyptian media personnel typically responded in a positive manner when questioned on the need to develop independent initiatives.

Perhaps with regard to Egypt's English-language press and international television news, such bootlegging is considered acceptable because of translation considerations. Regardless of the rationale, there seems to be little initiative being taken by the Egyptian media to decrease its dependency on Western news sources.

Cable News Network (CNN) in Egypt

When *Time* named Ted Turner as its 1991 Man of the Year, one phrase became CNN: "History as it Happens" (Henry, 1992). Certainly this was a mega-jump in stature from CNN's humble beginnings and the initial negative appraisal of Turner's venture. To many, he was simply, "The Mouth of the South." But, as Turner himself described his media positioning in the decade of CNN's development, "We paid our dues, went to every corner to get news and really got it for the Gulf war. CNN saw it and did something about it" (Turner, 1991).

Few could imagine the potential impact that CNN would have in the reporting of the Gulf war. Fewer still knew that for more than two years prior to the hostilities CNN had been negotiating with the Egyptian government to broadcast its 24-hour news service in Egypt. Mishinski (1990) has detailed this process and an analysis by Fahmy (1990) contributed to the perspectives of Egyptians anticipating electronic media incursions by the West. It is history that CNN was on the cutting edge of the Gulf war reporting and that its broadcasting became operational in Egypt at the same time. The impact of both circumstances became intertwined in a labyrinth of invective, condemnation, praise, and plaudits.

Newsweek described CNN's coup on the war's opening as "the most stunning sign yet of how that 24 hour network, the only one with truly global reach, is changing the news business forever. Indeed, the scoop was so timely perfect to the extent that some called January 16 'the night the networks died'" (Alter, 1990, 41). Some professionals were even more effusive, calling the Baghdad coverage "CNN's finest hour" ("CNN's Place...," 1991).

CNN's impact on the Gulf war coverage has been discussed by many (Anderson, 1991; Fore, 1991; LaMay, 1991; Larson, 1991; Leo, 1991; O'Heffernan, 1991; and Vincent, 1991). CNN's methods have been harshly criticized and its personnel tagged as a propaganda arm of Saddam Hussein ("Group...," 1991). On the other hand, President Bush stated that CNN was the primary source of news, information, and to-the-minute political intelligence for the U.S. government during the Crisis. "I learn more from CNN than I do from the CIA," Bush said (Henry, 1992, 15). Even General Schwartzkopf acknowledged its input as valuable (Alter, 1991).

Egypt's media, like most others, became dependent on CNN as a source for news gathering. The negative assessment of this situation was fully stated by Traber and Lee (1991), editorializing in *Media Development*:

> Media coverage of the Gulf Was was led by the US media, and to a lesser degree, the British and French. The rest of the world literally relied on a few powerful news organizations, primarily from the US, which had the technology and were favored by the military. And though the British media were part of the news pool, with privileged access to the theatre of war, no distinct British way of reporting was noticeable. The military superpower made sure that all the world's media became American.... The truth is that most Western media, with some honorable exceptions, accepted Washington's views and policy agenda on the kind of world and world 'order' it favours.... The

> final lesson from reporting the Gulf war pertains to the two-thirds world, better known as the Third World. Where were their voices? Where were their social actors? For most of the time there was only one actor: Saddam Hussein. All other voices were brought into the chorus of approval.... Government after government in the Third World was either brought or bullied into joining the coalition or keeping quiet. Those who did not felt the wrath of the American superpower.... The Third World has now lost its geopolitical significance and thus can be treated with disdain.... Not for decades has a situation existed in which the US media, having been cajoled and censored by the military, became a source of the world's news (1).

A strong position, and as described by Bagneid later in this section, Egypt's Radio and Television Union (ERTU) equally depended on resources directly from CNN with little modification or crediting. There is, of course, a deeper issue to consider when assessing the internal impact of such reliance. The focal point of the MacBride report, discussed in this work by Napoli, illustrates the issue: Western media dominance and imbalance of news flow are constraints that cannot be ignored.

Egypt became a key player in CNN's Global Village prior to the Gulf war. In 1988, Zuckerman (1988) gave an overview of what that role would entail. Those concepts did not go unnoticed in Egypt. An Egyptian holding company became Cable News Egypt (CNE). The outbreak of the Gulf war enabled it to become operational earlier than anticipated, and its service was distributed free of charge. Even those Egyptians who didn't know English turned to CNN. They did so to receive the visual images of developing war news, and out of curiosity because CNN's style is completely different from ERTU's. For those with any degree of English competence, there was a desire to learn the Western perspective on the war (Salama, 1991).

Though coverage may have been considered shallow, many Egyptians woke up on the dawn of January 17 to see and hear CNN's stories of the war in the Gulf. CNN's reports became a key means for the general population to keep abreast of developments. Of course, Egyptian broadcast and print media would become the backbone for public information follow-up.

There was, however, a significant difference between CNN's Egyptian broadcasts and those aired in other Gulf states, such as the United Arab

Emirates: CNN was broadcast in Egypt with no official censorship. The original agreement between the Egyptian government, CNE and CNN in June 1990 constituted provisional approval through the Higher Investment Authority and ERTU for satellite reception in Giza and TV transmission in Mokkatam. It was to be transmission without censorship of any sort.

Highly placed officials in Egypt projected the probable impact of CNN. As Mishinski reported, Hamdi Kandil, former Director, UNESCO's Division of Freeflow Information and Communication Policies, said:

> CNN has to be accepted as a Western biased news source. That is not to say that it is intentionally biased in its political views -- that there is a Zionist or capitalist plot. It is biased in terms of the sheer volume of information coming from the United Sates. And obviously volume carries something in its content.... We in the Third World are poor and don't have the means to communicate with each other. The Western media are powerful in terms of money and equipment (53).

Mishinski presented the low-key rationale for CNN's presence by Fathi El Bayoumi, former chairman of ERTU:

> CNN has been approved for investment as a tourism project because many tourists who come to hotels want to be in contact with what is going on in the world. Business people also. This is the main reason. The other people, or normal people, who don't know the language, they will see our news. So we are not much interested if the language is a barrier (53).

Kandil continued in a more positive vein:

> For those who will use it, CNN will enable them to keep in touch with the world in a way that they won't find in any other medium; they can listen to BBC, but television is different. However, this minority audience has always had access to what is going on in the world through foreign publications and travel (54).

CNE broadcast the CNN signal in Egypt on UHF channel 21 from December 1990 through March 1991. Though the hours of broadcast were greatly reduced from the 24-hour worldwide format, it must be remembered that the phenomenon was totally new to the Egyptian population. ERTU reported the following hours of CNN signal broadcasts:

December 1990		--	100 hours
January 1991	1 - 10	--	4 hours daily
	11 - 15	--	8 hours daily
	16 - 17	--	24 hours daily
	18 - 31	--	8 hours daily
February 1991		--	8 hours daily
March 1991		--	8 hours daily

The total hours broadcast by CNE during the war were the equivalent of almost two years' viewing of the 15-minute nightly ERTU English news.

Perceptions of CNN's Impact

During December 1991 interviews were conducted with leading Egyptian media professionals and academics. Their positions regarding the impact of CNN during and following the Gulf war are candid. There is a notably clear difference of opinion regarding CNN's "war" impact and speculation on its future. Following are excerpts from the interviews (Mohamed and Goueli, 1992):

> Samir El Touny (ERTU, Head of News Programs) -- This was the first time for the newsmakers to face competition from the Western channels. This stimulated the Egyptian journalists to do a better job. The news staff is trying hard to imitate CNN, depending on reports rather than just telling the news. Our reporters interview officials in the location of the events and comment on important events, such as happened in the Ukraine and the Peace Conference (in Madrid). Since we began receiving CNN, we tried to attract our viewers by using similar

techniques. We changed the news background using chroma and the monitors in the control room appeared, but this kind of imitation failed because we only have a few monitors in the news room. That's why the improvements looked awful.

Amani Kandil (ERTU channel 2, English Reader Editor) -- Egyptian television during the Gulf war realized that CNN began to attract its audience, so they made a news brief that broke up programs, and the correspondents' performance improved during this period.

Mahmoud Sultan (ERTU, Head of News Readers) -- CNN did not affect our news as it was expected to. We are still using slow rhythm, long introductions, unneeded shots, and we never go straight to the point. The order of the news items is the same since 1960, and some items take 5 - 10 minutes and even more. CNN makes news while we only comment on the event. Our correspondents do not cover the event. They either analyze, comment, or explain public reaction. We rebroadcast what we receive from CNN and similar channels. This differs drastically from what happens in CNN.

Abdou Mobasher (Journalist, Al-Ahram newspaper) -- During the Gulf war CNN proved to be essential. It proved and is continuing to prove that news has an audience who watch it. It also left a good impression about itself with its news and analysis, and created positive public opinion. One positive effect of CNN on the English news was the creation of the Visual News Center. It receives the news and transmits it directly. They also started to get live coverage from the location of the event.

Ismail El Nakib (Journalist, Al-Akhbar newspaper) -- The format (of ERTU) was affected; ranking of the news is a little better and also the time each item takes on air is less

Hussein Anan (Former Head, ERTU) -- It did not affect the news. It affected the peoples' -- who watched CNN --

understanding the Egyptian news and their credibility.

Heba El Semary (Faculty, Cairo University Faculty of Mass Communication) -- CNN helped the Egyptian newsmakers learn how news is made; thus, it began to report and introduce these reports by anchors. We should remember that CNN is an American network and this implies it presents Western viewpoints and it will never be totally objective. There must be some kind of censorship on these programs. We have to remember that we are in an Islamic country, and the illiteracy rate is very high. Therefore, their newsmakers should take these aspects into consideration when writing the news.

Morsi Attah-Allah (Chief Editor, Al-Ahram Al-Masai' newspaper) -- CNN's content should not exceed the limits of freedom allowed to the stations. It should also not curb the people's right of freedom.

Ahmed Omar Hashem (Professor, Al Azhar University and member of the People's Assembly) -- The most important point is that these stations do not violate our Islamic principles, our values, our traditions, or our freedom.

CNN had a moderate impact on ERTU's news format. Minor changes were made in style and method of presentation. The potential impact of CNN on the Egyptian population seems to stimulate a more intense reaction. The ongoing concern for the negative consequences of cultural imperialism, or media dominance, is clear. Yet that position is not consistent with other professional perspectives. Gehan Rachty, Dean of the Faculty of Mass Communication at Cairo University, noted that through CNN:

> We see democracy in action. We receive live news coverage and commentaries from democratic countries. We see foreign correspondents interviewing the U.S. President and other heads of State, asking them probing questions. It will impress upon us to ask questions and get answers from the government (Mishinski, 53).

The Foreign Community Assesses ERTU and CNN

A limited number convenience sample was employed for a survey of foreign media professionals in Egypt to provide a indication of this group's attitude toward ERTU and CNN coverage of Gulf war news (Abdulla, 1992). Results of this 27-item questionnaire provided the following comparison perspectives between ERTU's English news broadcast and CNN:

1) CNN's broadcaster's rhythm presentations were better.
2) CNN's content, style, and format seemed to be "better" news.
3) ERTU's anchors did not provide interpretations.
4) ERTU did not use live coverage, integrated coverage or continuous coverage of news items, whereas CNN did.
5) ERTU failed to capitalize on TV's "power of the picture."
6) ERTU depended on CNN as a resource; altered its format intensity; used more and visuals; and began to use an "update" format.

Abdulla concluded that "the coverage of Egyptian news on ERTU became more factual, more updated, used more diversified reports and more visuals. It also proved that, however, the positive effect was only temporary, for now that the CNN international signal is not available without subscription, the effect is not there anymore" (25).

Implications for the Future of CNN in Egypt

The aftermath of the Gulf war has left a strong imprint in media analysis and academic investigation has been intensive. Two major works have presented diverse views of Western media coverage of the Gulf war (LaMay, 1991 and Taber, 1991). The Egyptian point-of-view is clearly two-sided, with negative and positive considerations. Samir (1991) concisely presented these positions. The negatives:

1- CNN is an American network and audiences generally are exposed to American positions. The Global Village receives the American and Western point, regardless of what others think. (This point is supported by Ghareeb (1983), in the discussion of

American media coverage of Arabs. It is, he notes, a portrayal with "split vision.")

2- CNN will be biased toward news happening in the West, or of events which are in the American interest. Research has also confirmed the ability of the American media to "agenda set" and it is unlikely that Middle Eastern or other Third World news will be covered unless it is crisis coverage.

3- Egypt does not possess the technical facilities and/or expertise for international information dissemination. This perpetuates imbalance in the flow of information. (As Amin discusses in this work, even SpaceNet has severe limitations on its ability to counteract this.)

4- CNN makes the general public and media-government persons fear "cultural imperialism." The newly introduced network may attract viewers for the sake of news, but in addition, they will receive information, values, traditions, and meanings incompatible with traditional Arab culture and nationalism.

5- The presumed controlling impact of CNN over ERTU will make ERTU try to fit its format into the CNN mold. (A switched metaphor sees this as a David and Goliath battle with Egypt not having the capacity to compete.) In its attempts to be equal, ERTU will lose its identity and still not achieve a high level of competitiveness.

Yet Samir did see many positive effects:

1- Egypt will become a more integral part of the Global Village by being more tied to the technologically and economically advanced Western nations.

2- Competition will help the development of ERTU. Because of the CNN lead, ERTU made modifications of its style and format for news broadcasting during the Gulf war. The "new" formatting made it more in line with higher quality international formats.

3- The Egyptian population may develop broadmindedness by gaining a world view. CNN may contribute to reducing the media isolation of Egyptians.

4- Egyptian TV may be more obliged to report facts and

> perspectives, even those with negative overtones. It will not be the only source of information, and by being more "content competitive," will improve its credibility.

That CNN will have an overwhelming impact is not apparent at this writing. The initiation of CNN war broadcasts in Egypt was coincidence. As CNE already had obtained rebroadcast approval, the Gulf crisis only altered -- albeit dramatically -- the nature of its debut. The generalized effect on both average and elite Egyptians was precisely stated by S.A. Schleifer, Director of the Adham Center for Television Journalism at the American University in Cairo:

> CNN lost its novelty following the war. Before, it was available to everyone; people wanted to know so much what's going on it. But after the war, this was over; they knew what it is and were not interested anymore (Mohamed and Goueli).

The loss of the novelty is one thing; losses on a global scale may well be another issue. Elihu Katz (1992) of the Annenberg School for Communication at the University of Southern California has suggested that CNN's role in the Gulf crisis may have triggered "the end of journalism." CNN's "instant news" bypasses editorial review and inhibits journalistic analysis. The impact, he contends, is not only on the "American" media, but on the world. Broadcast and print media tried successfully to tell us about a war that was supposed to be, but:

> ...their failure to convince us is to their credit. The success of CNN is the symbol of this failure. From my point of view, it represents the beginning of the end of journalism as we have known it (9).

The Development of SpaceNet and its Impact

Hussein Amin

When ARABSAT was conceived in 1969, direct broadcasting service, often called community service, was envisioned as highly desirable for remote regions previously unable to receive television service. Despite seemingly great demand for such a service, it was never utilized during the years after the launches of the first two ARABSAT satellites. The development of the Egyptian International Television Network (SpaceNet), however, recently revived the dream of community service and served as a model for others.

This paper reviews the history of ARABSAT in Egypt before describing the establishment of SpaceNet. It then discusses the special role of SpaceNet in the Gulf Crisis.

The Development of ARABSAT

The Arab League was formed after World War II as a compromise between aspirations for Arab unity and for sovereignty for each of the 21 Arab States. The competing aspirations continue to be a factor in television program exchanges. The first Arab League mass media cooperation commenced in 1951 with the establishment of the Administration for Information and Publication to promote the Arab point of view internationally. The Permanent Committee for Arab Media was formed in 1960. In 1964, the Council for Arab Information Ministers first met. It was the forum with the highest Arab League media authority.

The 1967 war precipitated changes in patterns of communication in Arab countries, including Egypt. The war prompted a re-examination of the role of the media. This atmosphere saw the 1969 establishment of the Arab States Broadcasting Union (ASBU), a specialized agency of the League to coordinate radio and television efforts and train personnel (Boyd, 1982).

ARABSAT emerged at about the same time. Although Arab countries participated in INTELSAT (International Telecommunications Satellite) as early as its establishment in 1964, there was a desire to connect all Arab countries in a communication system to exchange cultural and educational television programs. The ASBU Engineering Committee gave the ARABSAT movement one of its first boosts by recommending space telecommunication technology. However, the Arab Telecommunications Union (ITU) added momentum by predicting substantial growth in communications development among Arab countries and the profitability of ARABSAT. UNESCO advised the movement on three occasions and recommended community television service among other proposals (Abu-Argoub, 1988).

In 1976, an agreement was signed to create an independent entity called the Arab Satellite Communication Organization within the Arab League jurisdiction. The goal of ARABSAT was to form an Arab space segment for public service for all members of the League. INTELSAT allowed ARABSAT's formation because it would cause no economic harm to INTELSAT and would complement or replace ground-based networks (Abu-Argoub, 1988). Members of INTELSAT are not allowed to set up their own satellite systems without permission.

ARABSAT members invested according to their means and interest. Now the 21 members include Algeria, Bahrain, Djibouti, Iraq, Jordan, Kuwait, Lebanon, Libya, Mauritania, Morocco, Oman, Qatar, Somalia, Sudan, Syria, Tunisia, the Palestine Liberation Organization, the United Arab Emirates, Yemen, Saudi Arabia, and Egypt (Amin and Murrie, 1992).

The ARABSAT organization includes the General Assembly, the Board of Directors, and the Executive Body. The Assembly, composed of Arab state ministers of telecommunications, is the highest authority. It includes non-voting members from ASBU, ATU, and the Arab League. The nine-member board includes five permanent members from those members who have invested the most. The Executive Body administers the operation (Abu-Argoub, 1988). However, ASBU is in charge of television program exchange which essentially represents policies of information ministries of Arab states.

Services include exchange of news and other programs, educational broadcasting (especially to remote areas), emergency communications, domestic telecommunications, and data transmissions including teleconferences, electronic mail, and newspaper publications (Al Saadon, 1990).

Al Saadon (1990) found that use of ARABSAT for television program exchange reflected the political, social and economic differences among Arab states. Those countries with better diplomatic relations were more likely to exchange programs. The stronger the country's economy, the more likely it exchanged programs using ARABSAT.

However, Al Saadon concluded that the introduction of the new satellite technology changed the media organizational attitude in the Arab world toward more cooperation and program exchange. Most Arab countries established exchange departments or are in the process of establishing them (Amin and Murrie, 1992).

The Egyptian International Television Network (SpaceNet)

Although Egypt's economy has its weaknesses, its diplomatic contacts, rich television tradition, and longtime involvement in program exchange set the stage for the development of SpaceNet when Egypt returned to the Arab League in 1988. At the time, the transponder for community television service was not used by either the League or by any Arab country to form the envisioned Arab International TVN community service (Amin and Murrie, 1992).

On December 6, 1990, the Egyptian Radio and Television Union (ERTU) signed an agreement with ARABSAT to lease bulk capacity of the direct TV broadcasting transponder 26 on ARABSAT satellite 1-A for 24 hours a day, seven days per week for three years starting from the first of November 1990 (Fayoumi, 1990). The lease could be extended with the approval of ARABSAT and ERTU. The annual fee was $2 million ("DTVB," 1990).

On December 12, 1990, SpaceNet started transmission with an average of 13 hours for daily programming including news, sports, entertainment, and religious, educational, and cultural programs to Arab countries and much of Africa, Europe and Asia (Khalil, 1990) (See appendix A).

The Role of the Egyptian SpaceNet in the Gulf Crisis

Although the Egyptian position in the Gulf Crisis was declared early on in the crisis, other countries' positions were not clear, i.e., Jordan's, Sudan's and Algeria's. That situation affected their public and caused confusion inside each state. The Iraqi media sensed the situation and decided to take advantage of it.

During the Gulf crisis, the Iraqi regime used the media for propaganda and intelligence purposes. They began by spreading external services to cover the Gulf area and various parts of the Arab world by utilizing a number of shortwave units they seized from Kuwait. In addition, the Iraqi regime began jamming most of the external signals coming to Iraq and Kuwait (Haggag, 1991).

The content of the Iraqi messages focused primarily on claims and issues such as the historical rights that Iraq has over Kuwait, and religious justifications for the invasion, and occupation of Kuwait. The latter was accomplished by generally portraying the crisis as a confrontation between Moslems and non-Moslems. Importance was also given to the imbalance of wealth between the rich Gulf states and the poor Arab countries. The Iraqi media also stressed the linkage between the liberation of Palestine and the withdrawal from Kuwait (Haggag, 1991).

Thus, Egyptian military troops in Saudi Arabia and Kuwait received basically their enemy's point-of-view for why there was a war. Only through SpaceNet services could this circumstance be reversed and Egyptian officials worked hard to initiate SpaceNet broadcasts. Their objective was simple: Egyptian messages for Egyptian soldiers.

Egyptian SpaceNet was the only Arab international television network operating during the Gulf crisis. It delivered Egyptian information to the Egyptian and Arab military forces deployed in Hafr El Baten in Saudi Arabia, in Kuwait, and in Shargha. Five TVROs (television receive-only downlink dishes) were installed in Hafr El Baten, Saudi Arabia. When the installations were fully operational, all Egyptian troops had easy access to programs from home.

ERTU also installed a TVRO to serve Egyptian military forces after they had advanced to assigned positions inside Kuwaiti territory.

ERTU installed a TVRO, a UHF TV transmitter of 1000 watts, and a 42-meter mast carrying a group of UHF antennas to direct the TV signal of SpaceNet among the Egyptian military forces in Shargha. When these troops advanced to the Rodum camp in Abu Dhabi, the equipment at Shargha was transferred to the new location (See Appendix B).

Strategies of the Egyptian SpaceNet During the Gulf Crisis

As an important and integral component of ERTU, SpaceNet followed ERTU strategies with regard to radio and television broadcasting during the

Gulf crisis. Although SpaceNet's broadcast schedule was a compilation of Egyptian television channels one and two (See Appendix C), SpaceNet was able to broadcast the news as it happened rather that waiting for scheduled television newscasts. ERTU established a news center to manage information and international news. This was helpful in providing news coverage from around the world that supported SpaceNet news and public affairs programs and helped to keep continuous coverage and follow up of the crisis.

Part of ERTU's strategy was to program its schedule according to the psychological mood of Egyptian and other Arab audiences during the Gulf crisis.

In terms of program content, SpaceNet coverage of the Gulf crisis reflected concerns arising from the different stages of the military campaign to liberate Kuwait.

During Phase One, the occupation of Kuwait from August 1990 to January 1991, programs consistently sought to reassure the viewing public that any problem between Iraq and Kuwait could be solved, but not before the Iraq's withdrawal to its own border. Other messages were that non-Arab countries would begin to interfere, a situation that was undesirable for Arab countries; that war was not the solution for the inequities in the distribution of Arab wealth; that joint projects and economic cooperation between Arab countries could better resolve this problem; and that the Iraqi claim that the crisis was a holy war was not justified. To drive home this last message, the point was stressed that no Islamic country would endanger sacred Islamic soil and expose it to foreign armies: Iraqi withdrawal from Kuwait was a must (Haggag, 1991).

During Phase Two of the crisis, the military operation from January 17, 1991, to the liberation of Kuwait on March 25, 1991, the main messages carried over SpaceNet were twofold: 1) that the refusal of the Iraqi president to negotiate would expose an Arab country to a war that would not only destroy it, but would also divide the Arab world, and 2) that the Arab world and international community would support, if they were not already participating, the joint operation to liberate Kuwait (Haggag, 1991).

Conclusion

It is clear that SpaceNet played a significant role during the Gulf crisis, whether on the level of the Egyptian armed forces who participated in the liberation of Kuwait or on the level of the Arab public in the Gulf. The greatest input was on the level of the armed forces. It provided the armed forces with an alternative to the media of the enemy. Before SpaceNet troops had been exposed to several months of propaganda from the Iraqis designed to lower troop morale. After SpaceNet began in December 1990, troops were made aware of their country's war effort as well as receiving news from home, thus raising morale and contributing to battle efficiency.

Radio broadcast also played a significant role during the Gulf war. ERTU strategy included: 1) using the multi-broadcast frequencies approach to overcome the Iraqi jamming; 2) utilizing some radio stations in Gulf states to retransmit Egyptian Radio programs carried via satellites which allowed a clear and powerful radio signal without any kind of interference; and 3) establishing two new radio services, The Voice of Kuwait and The Iraqi Free Voice, both transmitted to Iraq and Kuwait.

It is equally important to note that most Arab communication ministries and institutions granted direct access to televised information for the first time through the Egyptian SpaceNet, as it was the only source of helpful information in Arabic available in the Arab world throughout the Gulf crisis.

ERTU Broadcasting Responses to the Crisis

Magda Bagnied

When the Gulf war erupted, the Egyptian Radio and Television Union found itself generally unprepared for media crisis reporting. Granted, the ERTU ably functioned as a news gathering and disseminating agency. However, the combination of overwhelming international attention by the world media, coupled with the physical immediacy of events, placed pressure on ERTU to assume a leadership role for the Arab media.

With the Iraqi invasion of August 2, the ERTU Media Committee convened with the aim of crystallizing the media's political strategy for Egypt. The first decision was to establish a media operations room in order to plan, implement, and follow-up media directions for both radio and television.

It must be clearly understood that this was a major move for ERTU, as never before had an event necessitated such a response. Three major changes were made: 1) time allotted to radio and television news was increased; 2) formatting style was altered for broadcast news copy by allowing anchor interpretive comments and aiming interviews with subject experts and reports from field correspondents; and 3) the rhythmic flow of anchor presentation was adjusted.

Several technical improvements were also made. These included: 1) increasing the number of broadcasting frequencies to overcome Iraqi jamming; 2) strengthening the transmission wattage so as to cover the Gulf area; 3) picking up "Voice of Arabs" and re-transmitting it to reach new Arab states; 4) transmitting Egyptian radio and television specifically into Kuwait; and 5) transmitting the Egyptian SpaceNet to military troops in the Gulf states.

Starting January 12, 1991, the countdown began for the United Nations' acceptance of force as a possible tool to effect Iraq's withdrawal from Kuwait. ERTU decided to establish two broadcast rooms, one each for radio and television. Each was staffed by a full complement of personnel, including announcers, engineers, translators, special effects operators, and the like. Additionally, "air time" ready libraries with a one-week backlog were created; battle broadcast maps were composed; television and radio rooms shared news bulletins; the General Program of Radio Cairo was connected with all international television networks; and coordination was established between the broadcast rooms and the President's office and Minister of Information.

On January 17, ERTU cut regular broadcasting and made its first announcement of the beginning of the confrontation between Iraq and the Allied forces. As noted earlier in Weisenborn's discussion, CNN was now broadcasting on an ERTU channel. In a move to compete with the American news formatting of CNN, ERTU made several additional changes to both its technical and content modes. A special team was formed to edit verbal and visual battle news and all details of military operations were immediately broadcast.

Content became direct and focused on Egypt's role in liberating Kuwait, reminding listeners that the "burden of proof" was Saddam Hussein's and highlighting the destructive actions of Iraqi troops inside Kuwait.

As the battle was ending with the collapse of the Iraqi forces and Iraq's apparent readiness to withdraw its troops from Kuwait, the operations room directors held a meeting to review the political realities they presumed as the status quo. Media requirements after the battle and the liberation of Kuwait were also identified. The Minister of Information, Safwat El-Sherif, summarized that:

1) Egypt's swiftness in dealing with the crisis gave credibility to its Gulf and world policies and clarified Egypt's ability to move correctly during the crisis;
2) There was no Egyptian collusion with the "wrong-doers";
3) The complete collapse of Iraq was expected;
4) Regular broadcasts had constantly reminded Saddam that he was destroying all chances of ending the crisis peacefully.
5) The "Voice of Arabs" station would broadcast its transmission on 4 frequencies instead of 2, in order to reach all Arab states.
6) Saudi Arabia, United Arab Emirates, Qatar and Bahrain would allocate some radio frequencies to retransmit programs of the "Voice

of Arabs," so the Gulf states would be able to listen to Egypt's voice.

7) The monitoring section would undertake a major effort by working 24 hours daily, to monitor more than 20 broadcasting stations in one shift.

It is worth mentioning that radio monitoring was recorded amid frequency jamming by Radio Baghdad, which included all of Saddam's speeches, statements, conferences and the statements of the Revolution Leadership Council. The information collected by this effort was analyzed by the operations room minute by minute and helped develop ERTU's media strategy.

The Egyptian Radio Broadcasting presented through its news and political programs fourteen offerings, which included on the General Program, with You on-the-Air, the World on-the-air, Lights on the Events, Arab Horizon (a dialogue with a government official), Reports from Correspondents, the Press Says, Nation's Opinion, Egypt Today, A Window on Africa, etc. The General Program station presented more than one thousand political commentaries besides the Voice of Arabs commentaries.

On the Voice of Arabs program there were 7 programs such as: Names in the News, the Arab Journal, Tomorrow's Press, etc. The broadcasting station intensified dialogue with eminent Arab and Egyptian figures and Arab ambassadors, editors-in-chief of Egyptian and Arab newspapers; there were more than 4000 interviews. The Voice of Arabs also presented another program in collaboration with the Ministry of Foreign Affairs called, "With the Family in Kuwait," in order to make families in Cairo feel secure about Egyptians living in Kuwait.

During the Gulf crisis ERTU faced the situation efficiently by mobilizing its efforts and abilities in various ways. News networks in both radio and television were changed into a 24-hour main operations room. This was done to follow closely news coverage of the crisis on both the local and international level. There were different experts on call to provide explanations about crisis events. The Visual News Centre was established to provide a variety of international news sources. The center followed world news events through the French channel of C.F.I., the World Net, and CNN, besides programs from ARABSAT and Indian Satellite. The center was equipped with units to receive international news reports that came from television correspondents in some world capitals. Radio and television correspondents were utilized to cover most of the Arab capitals to intensify the news services. ERTU then introduced a news slot in the commercial network called, "The Middle East Panorama," from midnight to 3 a.m. It presented three news bulletins and two political commentaries. Transmission of the "Voice of Arabs" was extended to 24 hours and increased the number of news bulletins, news briefs and introduced new political and news programs.

Conclusion

Could ERTU compete with the highly trained and experienced Western media in its crisis coverage? Clearly not. But what is evident is that for the first time, an Arab-based national media system moved directly with speed to develop its own credibility with its own culture. Granted, there was the option for Arabs to receive Western radio and television. ERTU moved to provide a clear and preferred option: Arab peoples informed of events in their world by their media.

Egyptian Media: Newspaper

Hot or Cool Press Coverage of Iraq

Dina S. Lamey

The press in the Middle East tends to be closely merged with politics. Reporters are expected to reflect government views and limit criticisms of the government. They are expected to discuss issues from a position of commitment and that approach is difficult as they must state positions which do not necessarily reflect their true ideologies (Nasser, 1982).

Both the public and the government accept the role of the press as a tool of nationalism and politics in the Middle East. The standard press functions, entertaining and informing audiences, are replaced by sending mainly political messages which serve as propaganda for the centers of power and also in educating the masses. Arab leaders, in general, view the media as instruments for the advancement of national policy, devices by which the goals of the state are achieved (Rugh, 1979).

In Egypt the government confronts serious domestic and foreign problems that condition the manner in which it releases news to pressmen. Sensitivity to domestic public opinion as it reacts to certain major events, the impact of inflationary pressures and many other important national and international issues -- all -- impose restrictions on government informational mechanisms, and consequently, their relationship with the media (Koeppel, 1989).

Until August 2, 1990, the Iraqi leader was portrayed as a strong friend of Egypt and protector of the Arabs. But after that, President Hosni Mubarak called Saddam Hussein a liar for assuring him that he would not attack the tiny emirate. The word "liar" was the cue for the press. It then poured hatred and scorn on the Iraqi ruler, disclosing real and rumored crimes which were ignored when Mubarak and Hussein were good friends.

The purpose of this section is to investigate how the Egyptian press shaped news coverage of Iraq to align with government policies.

News of Iraq was isolated for study because the level of coverage has fluctuated dramatically since 1988 in response to Iraq's changing relations with Egypt. News coverage analysis of Iraq in the two major national newspapers, *Al-Ahram* and *Al-Akhbar*, and the opposition daily, *Al-Wafd*, is presented.

The topics reported are the gassing of the Kurds by the Iraqi troops in 1988, the 1989 Iraqi abuse of Egyptian laborers working in Iraq, the 1989 formation of the Arab Cooperation Council (ACC), and Iraqi public celebrations.

Events were chosen for this study to illustrate two issues: First, they show the presence, or absence, of Egyptian press freedom. Second, they illustrate the press' full support of government policies at times of important decision-making.

Research Data

The sample for this study consisted of 305 stories. These were divided among the three newspapers:

Al-Ahram	114 stories	37.4%
Al-Akhbar	140 stories	45.9%
Al-Wafd	51 stories	16.7%

Of the 305 stories used in the analysis, 204, or 68%, were from the pre-invasion time period. The remaining 101 stories, 32%, were from August 2, 1990, to January 15, 1991. The pre-invasion topic coverage is presented in Appendix D. The Kurdish issue received the least coverage with only 24 stories (7.9%): laborers' coverage was 79 stories (25.9%); 37 stories (12%) were of the Iraqi celebrations topic; and the ACC formation received the highest coverage with 165 (54.1%) stories.

Appendix D also contains the data in graph format for newspaper coverage comparisons for the pre- and post-invasion topic coverage and the valences of that coverage. Frequency is the total number of stories run by each newspaper for each of the four topics. Valence was determined by placing each newspaper article in one of three categories: positive, neutral or negative "attitude" perspective of the writing. The positive valence was for stories that had enchancement or complimentary statements, while the negative valence was presented in the opposite style, using criticism, rejection and the likes. Neutral valence was for those stories that stressed facts only.

The data illustrate that in all newspapers the predominant coverage for all topics was positive. Post-invasion was as presumed, as coverage switched to a neutral valence. Post-invasion topic frequencies was interesting in that for all newspapers coverage of the Egyptian laborers in Iraq increased dramatically. Coverage of the Kurd issue was present in all three newspapers, with 6 of the total being in *Al-Ahram*. Data for the Iraqi celebrations is not reported, as the post-invasion coverage in all three newspapers was non-existent.

Is there a factual base beyond percentage comparisons to ascertain if the newspapers altered both their coverage frequencies and story valence? To provide a justifiable answer chi-square tests were run on the topical coverage with pre-invasion stories being the "observed" frequencies and post-invasion stories being the "anticipated" frequencies. The standard X_2 statistic was used and all probabilities were set at alpha .05. Results of the chi-square values and their significant differences (s.d.) or non-significant differences (n.s.d.) for topic coverage and valence were:

Newspaper	Topic	Valence
Al-Ahram	s.d.	s.d.
Al-Akhbar	s.d.	s.d.
Al-Wafd	n.s.d.	s.d.

The n.s.d. forAl-Wafd topic coverage may be the result its being a weekly. Thus, the number of pre- and post-invasion stories might not have been sufficient enough for the rigor of the chi-square statistic. Nevertheless, the data indicate that there was a negative relationship between frequency of news item and valence. For the *Al-Wafd* no relationship was justified.

Discussion

This research contends that the Egyptian government does shape the news to gain public support for its policies. Even though there may be opposition, there is a certain demarcation beyond which the press, national and opposition, cannot go.

The two official newpapers *Al-Ahram* and *Al-Akhbar* displayed great similarity in content. They dealt with almost the same news stories and treated them with similar priorities. Even though much less coverage of the ACC was found in the *Al-Wafd*, the praise of the government for having taken that "wise" step could be clearly seen.

On the laborers' issue, the *Al-Wafd* gave the most outspoken criticism of the issue, attacking the government for not taking any measures to safeguard the laborers' financial and security rights, although Iraq and its leader remained immune to any criticism. The carefulness with which the topic was covered was also clear. The national papers concentrated on the money transfers issue rather than the deaths. The possibility that statistics of arriving dead bodies may have been falsely reported in the national papers would support this research position, that the government hid important facts from the public to continue gaining support for Egypt's relations with Iraq.

The issues that need further explanation, but were not the subject of this data analysis, are the press' abrupt change in position when the government decided to go against Iraq for its invasion of Kuwait. Why did previously suppressed news suddenly come to the surface? Why did the press not just condemn the invasion without having to appear double-faced and unstable? Questions such as these seem to be the crux of the "hot or cool" perspectives of the Egyptian press.

Foad Fawwaz, of the *Al-Wafd*, wrote on August 27, 1990, that in just a few weeks the Iraqi ruler changed from being a hero, defender of the Eastern Gate and the victorious champ who defeated the Arabs' enemy, into a killer, a vampire and the Arabs' Hitler.

Fawwaz argued that the violent tendencies of Saddam Hussein were not born with the invasion, that he was not an angel before that time. He noted that people everywhere, including the Arab world, knew of Hussein's bullying tendencies, but preferred to portray them in triumphant contexts. Fawwaz criticized the Egyptian government for having known all of Saddam's evils, but concealing them behind the cooperation agreement signed with Iraq. This was at the same time when "Saddam" was sending Egyptian laborers home dead to their families. The government, Fawwaz wrote, wanted good relations with Iraq and its leader, and hence gave legitimacy to his evils.

President Nasser once said that he wanted the people to know only what he thought they should know. To achieve this, he designated himself "the supreme educator of the Egyptian society" (Dabbous, 1982, 13). The Mubarak administration has continued to be the "educator."

Sensitive topics in Egyptian newspapers, including the opposition papers, have included Iraq's handling of its war with Iran, which was closely connected with its violation of human rights (using chemical weapons against Iranians and its own Kurds). Such topics were downplayed, and in most instances, not reported. Egypt at that time was keen on gaining Iraq's support as an important step towards reviving her political leadership in the Arab region. Furthermore, Iraq was providing jobs for thousands of Egyptians who "sent substantial earnings home" (Koeppel, 1989, p. 4).

It should come as no surprise that Egypt's press coverage was, and remains, tightly linked with government directives. So when certain events or developments in Iraq were government-supported, or viewed favorably, Egypt's press gave them similar backing. By the same token, when the Mubarak administration made a complete turn around concerning the very same events, the press followed suit almost blindly.

This research suggests that topics directly pertaining to Egypt's foreign policy are presented in line with government policies. Therefore, when Egyptian-Iraqi relations were good, coverage of Iraq tended to be strongly favorable and news harming that image was not present. On the other hand, when Egypt condemned Iraq's invasion of Kuwait, negative stories about Iraq were published and brutalities by Iraqi forces against Kurds and Egyptian labourers were disclosed to the Egyptian public.

In general, the role of Egyptian newspapers in political communication appears to be evolving with some rapidity, as are press relations with the government as regulator and supplier of news. In this context, the self-censorsip exercised by pressmen and gatekeepers as to whether they should editorialize their work, and the limits of such editorialization, will continue to be of particular importance.

Peripheral Vision as Newspapers Covered the Gulf War

James Napoli

Western "domination" of the global news system has become a truism that, from the perspective of the developing world, implies a reproof to the "Big Four" news agencies. By providing most of the international news published in the press of developing nations, Associated Press, United Press International, Agence France-Presse and Reuters are, the argument goes, helping to maintain a colonial relationship between the First World and the Third. Like other aspects of the Western culture "industry," the news agencies help to infuse their customers in the developing world with alien attitudes and values that serve to break down indigenous cultures while promoting expansionist capitalism. The upshot is to "recolonize" the developing world not only culturally, but in economic and social terms as well (Grcic-Polic 1989, 21).

A corollary of the media imperialism theory is that the press in developing countries is dependent on its once and current colonizers, specifically, France, Britain and what for years has been commonly considered the world's preeminent colonial media power, the United States (Tunstall 1977; Schiller 1971). Advocates of the New World Information Order adopted Galtung's (1979) "feudal structure," which describes the colonial relationship of the center nations (the North) over their respective peripheral nations (the South), to also describe the dominance of the big news agencies over their news colonies. The press in developing countries could not get information about the rest of the world except through the agencies, which provided a steady flow of stories mainly in one direction -- down. Any stories about developing nations that reached the outside world would, in turn, have to be filtered and distributed through news agency headquarters in London, Paris or Washington -- a fact that presumably reduced the authenticity of the Third World voice heard in the West.

A particularly insidious aspect of the imperialist scenario, in the view of its illuminators, is that Western control is not limited to "vertical" information flow. The neo-colonial system also ensures that "horizontal" flow of news between peripheral nations is stanched, or at least filtered; neighboring countries in the Third World, such as in sub-Saharan Africa and Latin America, hear little of each other except for what the centralized Western news agencies deign to provide (Meyer 1991). Indeed, it has not been unusual for people to get reports about major events in their own country from outside foreign, supranational news agencies. In explaining the impetus in the post-World War II era for starting a pool of news agencies for non-aligned countries, Pero Evacic wrote: "Even the small number of existing national news agencies in the developing countries... were reduced to passive recipients of information provided by the big information systems." Much of that information served, to paraphrase Masmoudi (1978), no interests or needs of the recipient countries.

Western critics have aggressively attacked the general theory of cultural "imperialism" as just a high-sounding pretext for government censorship. Indeed, even the relevance of the term "imperialism" to describe media processes and effects that are unforced and inadvertent has been challenged (Bertrand 1989). But even accepting an aspect of the argument, the assertion of "dominance" of the press in the Third World by Western news agencies, raises questions of responsibility. Is the developing world necessarily reduced to the position of "passive recipient" of global information? How much leeway does the press in developing countries have to change its state of dependence? And if that state of dependence is not changed, does the responsibility lie still in the "colonizing" news organizations -- or must the developing states and their media bear some blame for their continued victimhood?

To what extent have Egyptian media made efforts to be self-reliant in their reporting? Weisenborn (1979) studied the front page subject content of the *The Egyptian Gazette* during 1977-78. The *Gazette* is the English-language version of *Al Gomhureya*, one of the government papers. Using a data base of 61 sample editions, front page news stories were categorized by source of news, geographic area of coverage, and subject matter topics. Even though the *Gazette* is not representative of the complete Egyptian media, results are relevant as a basis for understanding the media dominance argument and giving it a Third World and Egypt perspective.

There were 735 news items in the analysis and over 75% were from Reuters, Associated Press, or United Press International. *Gazette* Special Services and the Middle East News Agency (MENA) reporting accounted for the remainder. A second study of the *Gazette* during 1988 reported no substantial differences in sources of news from the earlier study (Weisenborn, 1990).

An interesting contrast was made in the 1988 study through examining the *Korea Herald*, South Korea's main English language daily. Korea, like Egypt, experienced major "press freedom" changes in the early 1980's. A sample of 678 *Herald* news items illustrated sources of news markedly different from the *Gazette*. Associated Press and United Press International accounted for 39% of the total. Reuters was not a source for one news item. However, Korean Broadcasting and News Services provided 35% of the total, and special "stringer" reports were 26% of all stories. Clearly, even somewhat similar "developing country" presses differ in dependency on Western sources.

Other units of this research detail some of the reasons for the lack of independent Egyptian press and electronic media coverage. What may be all too evident is that technological ability, journalist training, and even editorial mandate are not the culprits. Napoli (1991) presented the position that the economic support of media and incentives to journalists may be reverse causality for Third World inabilities to produce their own coverage of events within their locales.

The scores of news agencies founded in and among developing countries suggest at least that these countries need not be utterly passive in their relationship with the West or with each other when it comes to gathering and disseminating news. Certainly the alternative news agencies have not been uniformly successful (Fitzgerald 1990), but their very existence provided some testimony that the "peripheral" countries could take the initiative to alter the colonial relationship to their advantage. Further, whatever passivity comes of being a dependent in a neo-colonial relationship presumably can be overcome as the resources and means become available for the press in developing countries to conduct its own reporting in other "peripheral" nations, as well as in the West. The seminal 1980 UNESCO report by the International Commission for the Study of Communication Problems -- the MacBride report -- stresses the importance of an increased role of journalists in developing countries as a precondition for adequate presentation and interpretation of events from various parts of the world:

> They must have expanding possibilities for the coverage and distribution of reports about their own countries; they should be in a position to counteract the bias sometimes contained in stories which only present western perceptions of distant realities; at the same time, they should have more opportunities to report and interpret international affairs from their particular vantage points (149).

In a sense, the 1991 Gulf war provided an elegant test case to determine the extent to which the press in a "peripheral" country, Egypt, would successfully assert its independence from the foreign media, particularly from the international news agencies, if given the opportunity. Iraqi President Saddam Hussein certainly provided the Egyptian press with a motive for extensive independent news coverage.

The invasion of Kuwait by Iraqi forces on August 2, 1990, was itself interpreted as a direct slap at Egypt, since Egyptian President Hosni Mubarak had just passed on to the emir of Kuwait Iraqi reassurances that Saddam would not attack. President Mubarak was furious with what he perceived as Saddam's double cross, and said so in a press conference on Cairo radio August 8 (Lesch 1991, 38). In a country where the president indirectly sets the news agenda for the semi-official press, the cue for extensive coverage was unmistakable. Further, many Egyptian interests were at stake. On the political front, Egypt feared that Iraq's invasion would overturn the regional balance of power and militarily threaten its other vulnerable neighbors. And, of course, the invasion had many negative economic impacts on Egypt, including a substantial loss of remittances from its workers in foreign countries, reduced revenue from the Suez Canal and tourism, the elimination of development assistance from Kuwait and trade with Iraq, and the loss of bank deposits in Iraq and Kuwait. One estimate put Egypt's economic losses at $9 billion (Lesch 1991, 39). Though these costs were eventually offset from other sources, the immediate economic consequences of the invasion seemed dire indeed. As a news story in Egypt, the invasion of Kuwait could only have been bigger if Egypt itself were invaded. As it turned out, Egypt did the invading. It sent about 40,000 troops to Hafr El Baten in Saudi Arabia to join the U.S.-led military coalition that liberated Kuwait in a ground assault that began Feb. 23, 1991.

The fact that the ground war was launched from a nearby Arab country with which Egypt was on reasonably good terms -- Saudi Arabia -- created an ideal situation for direct horizontal coverage of another "peripheral" state. That is, the Egyptian press was in a position to minimize its dependence on Western news agencies by providing coverage of the war with its own reporters, who seemingly had some advantages over their Western counterparts. The war, after all, took place in Egypt's back yard, and belligerents on both sides shared a common language, religion and culture. Further, the Egyptian press -- at least the government-supported semi-official press (as distinct from the opposition press) -- had the resources to do an exceptional job of news coverage. *Al-Ahram*, the most prominent and venerable of Egypt's Arabic-language newspapers, is the flagship in a flourishing empire of newspapers and magazines. It has an enormous news staff with an extensive foreign bureau system, as does its chief rival, the somewhat less ponderous daily *Al-Akhbar* and weekly *Akhbar al-Yom.* The weekly has the largest circulation of any Arabic newspaper in the world; both *Al-Ahram* and *Akhbar al-Yom* have substantial circulations in much of the Arab world, including Saudi Arabia. Presumably, the Egyptian press did not need to rely heavily on the filtered reports of the war distributed vertically through news services in Washington, Paris and London if it chose not to rely on them. It was in a position, to use the language of the MacBride report, "to counteract the bias" of Western perceptions of the news and to "report and interpret international affairs from their particular vantage points." But to what extent did it do so?

Egypt's Press Goes to War

As discussed later in this volume by Dabbous, government, as well as opposition -- newspapers approached the gulf situation differently. To establish a basic idea of the general nature of government newspaper coverage, two content analyses of front page news item coverage were completed for *Al-Akhbar* and *Al-Ahram*, both government newspapers, from Jan. 17 to March 22, 1991.

Figure 1 reports the analysis for topical areas of coverage: Local, or Egyptian; Arabic, Gulf States; and Foreign. While local news items were identical for both newspapers at 36%, distinct differences are noted in both Arabic and foreign coverage. *Al-Akhbar* contained more than twice the

Fig.1
Front Page Coverage Comparisons of *Al-Akhbar* and *Al-Ahram* Newspapers
January 17 - March 22

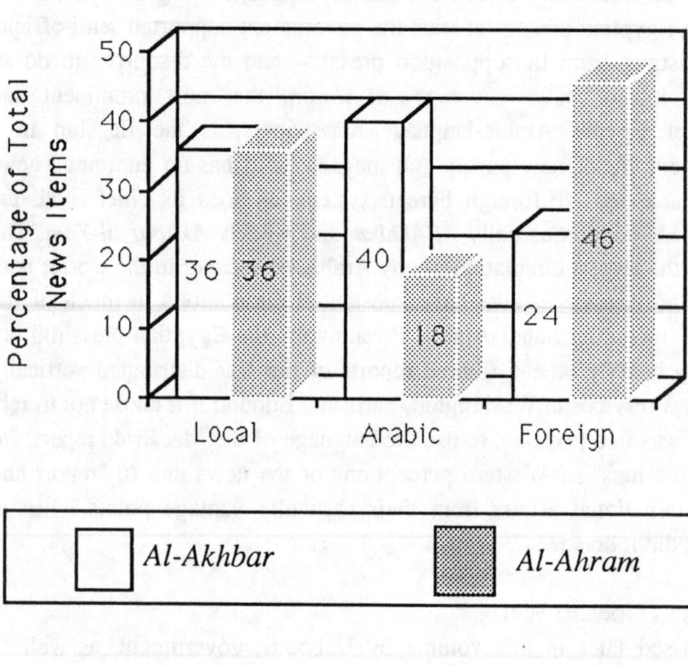

Fig. 2
Front Page Coverage Comparisons of *Al-Akhbar*
and *Al-Ahram* Newspapers
January 17 - March 22

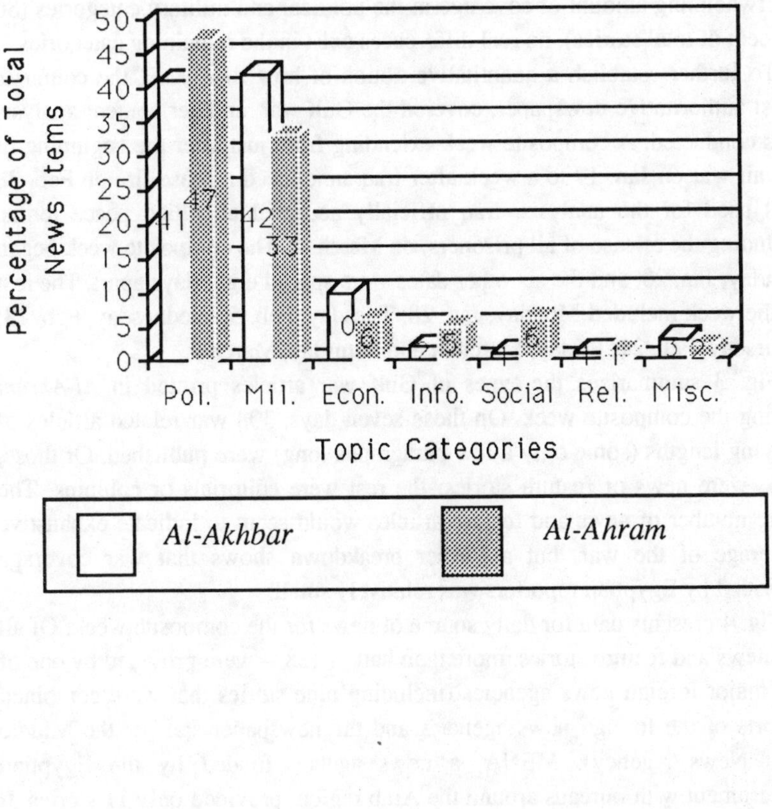

number of Arabic stories and *Al-Ahram* was almost twice as heavy in reporting foreign news stories. One might ask whether such data reflect a pro-Arab bias of *Al-Akhbar* and a pro-West bias of *Al-Ahram*.

A more detailed analysis of the subject categories suggests that while the areas of coverage may have been quite different, the actual coverage of subjects was not. Of the categories identified in Fig. 2 -- political, military, economic, informative, social, religious, and miscellaneous -- only reportage of military issues was noticeably different. In that category *Al-Akhbar* exceeded *Al-Ahram* by 9 stories, or roughly 30%. And, given the overwhelming amount of coverage in the political and military categories (80 percent of total stories), no real differences exist in the remaining categories.

To further establish a quantitative notion of how *Al-Ahram*, the country's most authoritative newspaper, covered the Gulf war, another content analysis was conducted. A composite week extending from just after the beginning of the air war on Jan. 17 to a week after Iraq announced a cease fire on Feb. 28 was used for the analysis. Iraq officially accepted all allied peace terms, including the release of all prisoners, on March 4. The composite week began Sunday, Jan. 20, and the six other dates were spaced eight days apart. The rest of the week included Monday, Jan. 28; Tuesday, Feb. 5; Wednesday, Feb. 13; Thursday, Feb. 21; Friday, March 1; and Saturday, March 9.

Fig. 3 summarizes the types of Gulf war articles printed in *Al-Ahram* during the composite week. On those seven days, 308 war-related articles of varying lengths (some only a few paragraphs long) were published. Of those, 256 were news or feature stories; the rest were editorials or columns. The large number of news and feature articles would seem to indicate exhaustive coverage of the war, but a further breakdown shows that war coverage provided by Egyptian reporters was relatively small.

Fig. 4 presents data for daily source of news for the composite week. Of all the news and feature stories, more than half -- 138 -- were provided by one of the major foreign news agencies (including nine stories that were combined reports of the foreign news agencies and the newspaper staff or the Middle East News Agency). MENA, a news agency funded by the Egyptian government with bureaus around the Arab region, provided only 11 stories. It is noteworthy that a relatively high dependence -- over 50% -- of the Egyptian press on foreign agencies for international news also was established in a 1984 comparative study involving a number of other developing countries (Haynes 1984).

Fig. 3

Date	Editorial	Column	News	Features	Total
Jan. 20	2	7	63	1	73
Jan. 28	2	3	36	4	45
Feb. 5	2	6	38	5	51
Feb. 13	---	10	29	---	39
Feb. 21	2	5	27	1	35
March 1	1	4	25	6	36
March 9	1	7	21	---	29
Total	10	42	239	17	308

Type of Gulf war-related articles in *Al-Ahram*

Fig. 4

Date	Foreign Wire	MENA	Staff (Egypt)	Staff (Foreign)	Wire/ Staff	UNK.	Total
Jan. 20	22	4	15	11	3	18	73
Jan. 28	23	1	4	8	1	8	45
Feb. 5	22	1	10	11	---	7	51
Feb. 13	23	1	3	3	2	7	39
Feb. 21	14	2	2	7	1	9	35
March 1	15	1	3	7	2	8	36
March 9	10	1	6	5	---	7	29
Total	129	11	43	52	9	64	308

Source of articles on Gulf war-related topics in *Al-Ahram*

Of all the war-related articles, including opinion pieces, 95 -- or about 30% of the total -- could be identified as having been written solely by staffers or correspondents. But of those, all but a handful were written either from within Egypt or from places other than Saudi Arabia, where the Egyptian army was located. The front-line coverage of the war by *Al-Ahram* correspondents in Saudi Arabia for the composite week consisted of six stories. Purely on the basis of numbers of articles, then, less than 2% of the war coverage in *Al-Ahram* came from its own correspondents in a neighboring country where the world's biggest story of the year, a conflagration directly involving thousands of Egyptian troops, as well as other Egyptian vital interests, was being staged.

The quantitative findings were consistent with information provided in an interview with Hassan Fouad, who helped direct the war coverage as deputy editor-in-chief of *Al-Ahram*. The newspaper had no bureau or full-time correspondent in the Gulf at the time of the invasion, Fouad said, and most stories it received from the Gulf at the time of the Iraqi invasion were provided by foreign news agencies. The newspaper did have contact with a few free-lancers and *Al-Ahram* staffers on leave of absence on newspapers in the United Arab Emirates, Bahrain, Qatar and elsewhere. These people would sometimes send stories to be published in Egypt. However, no one from Al-Ahram was sent to cover the war in its entirety. Occasionally, writers who cover military affairs were sent on "special missions" to the gulf -- for three or four days at a time -- to cover the war.

The thinness of the staffing apparently was reflected in the thinness of the content. Fouad said *Al-Ahram* reporters were given little access to the field and generally were not allowed to travel with the Egyptian army. Ministry of Defense officials arranged all travel and accompanied reporters everywhere they were allowed to go. In addition to direct military censorship, "arrangements" usually were made by the Ministry of Defense to control the access of reporters to sources of information and thus to prescribe the content of their dispatches. Reporting on the war -- and on military affairs in general since Nasser's time -- by the newspaper's staff was little more than relaying press releases. By the same token, MENA was used by the newspaper mainly to confirm "official" government positions and generally provided weak war coverage, Fouad said.

Under the circumstances, it is not surprising that the newspaper depended so heavily on foreign news agencies and other outside sources for news of the war. In fact, dependence on the outside -- Western -- media by *Al-Ahram* was even more pronounced than the numbers from the content analysis indicate. Not only did the paper run a substantial amount of foreign news agency material, but many stories written by the newspaper's staffers were drawn directly from coverage provided by Ted Turner's CNN. Journalists in Cairo were assigned to monitor CNN for new developments during the average eight hours a day the network was broadcast in Egypt during the war. Further, *Al-Ahram* correspondents in Washington, where CNN was available 24 hours a day, frequently wrote and sent stories based directly on the latest bit of war news they saw on television. "CNN was even more helpful than the wires," Fouad said.

A similar situation existed at *Al-Akhbar* and *Akhbar al-Yom*, though an apparently more sustained effort was made to provide independent reporting. Tours of the front and the Egyptian troops were organized by the military, and stories were read by military censors, but reporters and photographers sent by the newspapers did manage to produce a substantial number of articles, including features about how the ordinary Egyptian soldier was faring in the field, according to Said Sonbol, editor-in-chief of the newspapers during the war. He said the military was generally cooperative, though they "don't appreciate the time and urgency" of a newspaper's need to get a story approved quickly: "Every minute and second was important."

Farouk El Shazli, chief military correspondent for the newspapers, maintained he was allowed to roam freely among the Egyptian forces and could dictate stories over the telephone directly from the field to the newspaper without censorship. But El Shazli, who has been covering military affairs for 32 years, acknowledged that he and the other reporters were "all very well trained about what to say and not to say." He was with the Egyptian troops -- and CNN -- when they entered Kuwait. But, consistent with Egyptian government policy to go no further once Kuwait had been liberated, El Shazli and his colleagues did not accompany other allied forces into Iraq to cover the war's aftermath. The Egyptian journalists went home a few days after the cease fire despite other major news stories unfolding, including more fighting in Iraq and rehabitation and domestic turmoil in Kuwait.

Egyptian journalists did not seem to have enjoyed any special privileges or access because they were Arab allies in Saudi Arabia. In fact, Fouad observed that American and European reporters -- who complained bitterly of military restrictions during the gulf conflict -- had been given more of a "free hand" by the Saudis than was given to Egyptian reporters. "CNN was on the spot, but we didn't have this privilege," he said. No satellite was available to Egyptian television crews to transmit stories directly to Cairo; broadcasters generally had to wait until they got back to Egypt to file their footage, which may help account for its paucity on Egyptian television. Further, though Egyptian involvement in the ground war may have been a relatively minor consideration for most of the Western press, first-hand stories on the Egyptian forces did appear outside the country, often in spite of attempts to enforce censorship. Among them were pieces filed by Forrest Sawyer of ABC News, Tony Horwitz of *The Wall Street Journal* and Chris Hedges of *The New York Times* (Hedges 1991).

Covering the Arab World

Egyptian editors interviewed for this study said they thought their newspapers did as good a job as they could covering the Gulf war under the circumstances. But the circumstances were not conducive to good coverage. The problem, they noted, was not just logistics or military censorship, but the lack of Egyptian newspaper bureaus and dependable, full-time correspondents with good contacts in the gulf, or, for that matter, anywhere else in the Arab world. As previously noted, *Al-Ahram* and *Akhbar al-Yom* circulate in the gulf, including Saudi Arabia and Kuwait, and in other Arab countries. Millions of Egyptians work throughout the Arab world, including Iraq, Kuwait and Saudi Arabia. But in spite of that broad circulation area and an avid readership market of expatriate Egyptians, the major Egyptian newspapers rely heavily on Western news agencies -- and now CNN -- for news of their own region, a dependence made painfully obvious by their own staffs' sparse front-line coverage of the Gulf war. The only correspondent *Al-Akhbar* had in Baghdad was a reporter for an Iraqi newspaper, which, like the rest of the news media in Iraq, was a propaganda arm of the government. He had done some writing for the Egyptian newspaper, but stopped filing when the war started. No one was sent from Cairo to do the job. *Al-Akhbar* had no Peter Arnett to call its own.

It seems particularly ironic that there are no Egyptian newspaper bureaus in any other Arab country when one considers the number of Egyptian bureaus in the West. Between them, *Al-Ahram* and *Al-Akhbar* have bureaus -- in most cases they duplicate bureaus -- in Washington, New York, London, Paris, Rome, Athens, Bonn and Moscow. That's a tremendous investment of resources to cover, using Galtung's terminology, the "center" nations of the West instead of the "peripherals" in the Arab world. There seem to be two principal reasons this is the case, both centering on conditions that prevail among Arab nations rather than "imperialist" pressure from outside news organizations.

First, as editors from both *Al-Ahram* and *Akhbar al-Yom* confirmed, volatile political relations among Arab countries themselves discourage the newspapers from establishing a bureau system or assigning permanent correspondents to cover the Arab world independent of the reputedly innocuous, official MENA bureaus. "It's not a matter of money," said Hassan Fouad. "But if one day a bureau is open, another day it is closed." It all depends on the nation's current foreign policy toward Egypt and, historically, foreign policy in the region can be fickle. The 1991 Gulf war was only the most recent event to splinter regional loyalties.

Egypt's bilateral relations with countries within the Arab world, particularly since the 1952 Nasserist revolution, have often been strained. The Free Officer regime was at the outset aggressively occupied with the politics of the Middle East in its bid to assert a regional leadership role. This brought it into conflict with other Arab states, notably Saudi Arabia, Jordan, Iraq and Syria. Egypt's revolutionary nationalism and its concerted effort to subvert conservative states made Egypt's news media an unwelcome presence in countries that were the focus of Egyptian subversion. "The Voice of the Arabs" radio station and the more traditional "Enemies of God" radio program "poured invective not only on the imperialists but more directly upon those leaders in the Arab world considered to be their agents, viz., the Saudi ruling house, the various shaykhs and rulers in the Gulf states" (Vatikiotis 1991, 405). Another particularly difficult period for Egypt's relations with other Arab states took place after President Sadat signed the peace treaty with Israel, a move that lead to the virtual breakup of the League of Arab States and the severing of diplomatic relations with Egypt by several Arab states (Vatikiotis 1991, 435). Although President Mubarak was able to some extent to bring Egypt back into the Arab fold, Egypt's history of militant nationalism and of making peace with the hated Israeli "entity" were not forgotten by other Arab states. Founding an Egyptian newspaper bureau within another Arab nation's borders thus would be looked upon with suspicion, and the bureau's position there always would be tenuous, according to editors interviewed.

The mutual distrust between Egypt and its Arab allies surfaced after the war in the gulf media, which, from Egypt's point of view, played up the role of American and gulf forces in liberating Kuwait, while minimizing that of Egypt and Syria (Fouad 1991, 23). Further strain became evident after the gulf countries drastically reduced the support they pledged for Egypt and Syria to participate in the post-war security arrangement. When Egypt subsequently decided to withdraw its forces in protest, the gulf countries seemed unconcerned, raising further Egyptian resentment. That resentment was manifested in the Egyptian press as a "campaign of criticism" against the presumed ingratitude and haughtiness of gulf leaders (Fouad 1991).

There was a second reason -- beyond unstable Arab relations -- to explain why the leading Egyptian newspapers chose to establish bureaus in the West rather than in other Arab countries: news. Religiously conservative gulf states like Saudi Arabia and militant secular states like Iraq and Syria tightly control coverage from the outside first by limiting access of foreign journalists to their countries by selectively denying visas. And, even if journalists are allowed into the countries, their movements and access to information are strictly controlled. As a result, said *Al-Akhbar*'s Said Sonbol, the region ordinarily produces "no big news." The closed nature of most Arab societies thus makes it more attractive to concentrate on U.S. and European capitals, where foreign journalists can "operate in a more easy and free way" -- producing more news of interest to Egyptian readers.

Government constraint and censorship define the norm for the Arab press. With the exception of Lebanon, even those countries with the freest press systems, Kuwait and Egypt, are tightly bound by government in many respects (Koeppel 1988; Napoli 1992). In closed societies like Saudi Arabia, where newspapers for three days did not inform their readers that Iraq had invaded neighboring Kuwait, the press characteristically waits for government handouts before printing any sensitive material (Franklin 1991). Editions of foreign newspapers, including *Al-Ahram*, can be and have been prevented from coming into the country for carrying even the most mildly unflattering story about a member of the royal family -- or an advertisement showing a woman with bare shoulders or legs.

Summary and Conclusions

This research assumed that the major Western news agencies largely dominate international coverage provided by newspapers in the Arab world, as in much of the rest of the developing world. An examination of the newspaper coverage provided by the major Egyptian newspapers of the 1991 Gulf war did nothing to dispel the "media imperialism" theory. Indeed, the content analysis found that a heavy percentage of news stories published about the war in *Al-Ahram* was from foreign news services, as well as from a major new factor in the international news mix, CNN. Further, the content analysis, as well as interviews with editors and reporters at *Al-Ahram* and *Al-Akhbar* newspapers, tended to confirm that front-line coverage of the war by staff on the Egyptian press was extremely thin. This was attributed partly to a larger problem, the lack of Egyptian news bureaus and full-time correspondents in the gulf and elsewhere in the Arab world, even though the newspapers do have a substantial number of news bureaus in the West.

In terms of resources, the Egyptian press could provide greater coverage of the Arab world -- the "peripheral" states in the Middle East. But it does not. The fault -- to use a judgmental word implied in much of the rhetoric of the imperialism theorists -- cannot be attributed solely to Third World passivity in the face of overwhelming Western media domination. Constraints within the Arab world itself play a significant role in limiting coverage. Volatile political relationships among Arab states and the culture of control pervading the region have discouraged the Egyptian press from aggressively and comprehensively reporting on the rest of the Arab world. When the Gulf war broke out, it was simply easier to continue its reliance on Western news agencies to provide most of the coverage, rather than to use the sheer magnitude of the event as fortuitous pressure to change a debilitating pattern of dependence.

Western hegemony over the global media system may continue for years to come, but certainly Arab countries already are in a position to begin, again in the words of the MacBride report, to "counteract the bias" of Western perceptions of news events. The recent founding of a non-government, regional television network, the Middle East Broadcasting Center, is testament that passivity is not inevitable. MBC, which is backed by Saudi investors, beams uncensored news via satellite throughout the Arab world from studios in London. Its intensive, balanced news coverage is reportedly gaining big audiences in a potential market of 300 million Arab viewers (Ibrahim 1992). The experience of Gulf war coverage also invites suggestions on how to open opportunities for all Arab journalists, but particularly in print, to enhance coverage of regional events from their own vantage points.

First, Arab states must not allow the vagaries of regional political alliances and antipathies to interfere with news coverage. As far as Egypt's major newspapers are concerned, there seems to be no prospect of establishing a bureau system to cover the region as long as they feel that an abrupt change of policy could just as abruptly render their correspondents personae non gratae, and their bureaus closed. Arab states serious about improving regional news coverage while reducing the dependence of Arab media on Western agencies can publicly commit to tolerating newspaper bureaus from elsewhere, regardless of other considerations.

Second, internal censorship and control of foreign correspondents must be greatly moderated in virtually every Arab state. Part of the reason that Egypt's major newspapers have put their resources into sending correspondents to the West instead of to other nations on their own periphery is the government-imposed straightjacket on news reporting throughout the Arab world. Until access to information is improved, little reportage can be done that would distinguish itself from that already provided by Western news agencies.

Egypt seems not to have been alone in missed opportunities to develop its press. Nain (1991), in reporting on the effectiveness of the Malaysian press in Gulf war coverage, noted that "what is evident... is that the Malaysian mainstream press, preoccupied as they were with towing the official line or providing an ethno-religious angle on the conflict, lost a valuable opportunity to educate the Malaysian public" (31).

And third, newspapers in the region must plan now how they will cope with the new challenge from the likes of CNN, which played such a disquietingly prominent part in news coverage of the Gulf war. Egypt's newspapers are traditionally strong on analysis, an advantage the print media have over television. In fact, *Al-Ahram* has a center for strategic and political studies that helped provide a steady stream of expert commentary during the war, albeit from the comfort of newspaper and academic offices in Cairo. But the newspapers cannot give up the field of reporting to television without damaging their own relevance -- a problem that affects the print media in the West as well as in the Middle East. Robert Fisk (1992) of *The Independent* in London noted that the Gulf war and the omnipresence of television cameras woke him up to the urgent new task to redefine the role of print journalism. Newspaper reporters who merely watch CNN to relay what's happening at the moment are turning their publications into mere "appendages of television,"

Fisk wrote. They are abandoning the tasks of description, investigation and first-hand news analysis, which can be done more effectively, and with less susceptibility to official manipulation, in print than on television. Arab newspapers that don't play to those strengths, and that rely too heavily on international television networks for the news, will merely succeed in developing a new line of dependence on the West.

Note

My thanks to those Egyptian journalists, particularly those mentioned in the text, who agreed to be interviewed on the Gulf war coverage for this paper. I am also grateful to AUC graduate student Sahar Hegazi, who coded *Al-Ahram* for the content analysis, and to undergraduate Nagla Nofal, who tabulated the results.

Comparisons of National and Opposition Press Coverage

Sonia Dabbous

On August 2, 1990, Iraq invaded Kuwait, dividing almost the entire world in two camps: the Iraqi army on one side and United States troops supported by 28 nations on the other.

At the beginning of the invasion, almost all Arab countries condemned the invasion, but after the foreign troops arrived in Saudi Arabia, points of view within the Arab World began to differ. This was evident among states and within individual countries. A clear example is the case of Egypt. In Egypt, where a multi-political-party system prevails, differences of opinion were apparent between the National and the Opposition (or party) presses. These were reflected in the following newspapers: *Al-Ahram*, *Al-Akhbar* and *Al-Gomhureya*, which constitute the three major national newspapers; and *Al-Ahali*, *Al-Shaab*, *Al-Wafd*, *Al-Ahrar*, which constitute the major opposition newspapers.

At the beginning of the crisis, all opposition party papers in Egypt seemed to agree on one stand. They condemned the Iraqi invasion of Kuwait and asked for a solution within an Arab diplomatic context. When an Arab diplomatic solution wasn't effected and non-Arab troops began to move to the Gulf area, a wide range of positions developed.

These differences were reflected in press opinions presented. Editorial questions posed by National and Opposition presses during the period of the actual military operation centered around the following types of issues: Should foreign interference in Arab affairs be allowed? Should Moslems accept non-Moslem troops fighting and killing their co-religionists? Were the decisions of the Arab Summit held in Cairo fair?

An overview of Egyptian press laws presents the political and legal conditions prevailing at the start of the war. A content analysis of the front pages of *Al-Ahram* (national daily), *Al-Wafd* (opposition daily), and *Al-Shaab* (opposition weekly) was conducted covering the period of military operations, January 14 to February 28, 1991. The research uses the extent, direction and subject categories of front page news items about the Gulf war.

Political and Legal Environments

After the 1952 revolution, the political evolution from the single-party to multi-party system could be divided into two phases: first, from July 1952 until November 1976, and second, from November 1976 until today. 1952 marks the year of the revolution which transformed Egypt into a Republic with a single-party system, while 1976 marks the issuance of the People's Assembly law permitting the establishment of political parties based on concrete political programs.

Six political parties currently function in Egypt, each with a newspaper to represent its views. These are: The National Democratic Party with Mayo newspaper; the New Wafd Party with *Al-Wafd* newspaper; the Socialist Labour Party with *Al-Shaab* newspaper; the Al-Ahrar Party with *Al-Ahrar* newspaper; The Tagammo' Party with *Al-Ahali* newspaper; the Ummah Party with *Al-Ummah* newspaper.

Today freedom of opinion and expression is included in varying forms in the constitutions of nations with widely differing political and press systems. While some constitutions guarantee freedom of speech, others mention only freedom of the press.

Freedom of speech in Egypt has two bases -- constitutional and judicial. The constitutional base is divided in two phases. The first deals with the constitutional foundation for providing freedom of speech through the newspapers. It states that the press is free within the boundaries of law, that censorship of newspapers is forbidden, as is the suspension of any paper (Items 14 and 15 of the Constitution). The second deals with constitutional restrictions on the freedom of speech "necessary for the protection of the social system" (Item 15 of Constitution).

With the death of Nasser in 1970, a new climate was the emergence of Sadat's style of government. After the 1973 war and political infitah, a new political direction for the press became apparent. One press law was Number 4 for 1975 to establish the Higher Council for the Press. The council protects reporters' freedom of expression and opposition.

In 1977 the right to establish political parties was embodied in the Law 40 issued by the National Assembly. This law gave each party the right to issue a newspaper to express its opinion without being restricted to a license.

Sadat failed to provide the democratic atmosphere for the political parties to operate, and by September 1981, closed all the opposition papers and imprisoned many of the leaders of the opposing parties. The press in this period lost the degree of freedom it had enjoyed and was turned into a state-controlled instrument for managing public opinion. This climate would exist well into the administration emerging after Sadat's assassination. Mubarak's administration then freed imprisoned opposition leaders and gave opposition parties the freedom to operate again.

Considering these political and legal conditions, we can now say that there are two press theory models functioning at the same time in Egypt. There is the authoritarian model represented by the national press aiming at interpreting the official point of view; and on the other hand, the social responsibility model is represented by the opposition press. Within the opposition press there are moderate and extremist papers, depending on the extent of their deviation from the government views.

The Newspaper Analysis

This coverage analysis is derived from three papers, *Al-Ahram*, *Al-Wafd* and *Al-Shaab*. It is a period of six weeks from January 14 until February 28, 1991, inclusively (the actual war period). Since the front page is the mirror of a newspaper that reflects major events, discussion is limited to the examination of only the front page. Headline photos, cartoons and advertisements were not included.

The content analysis categories were classified as:

<u>Number of Stories</u>: Classifying the total number of news stories on the front page into two categories: The total of stories and the number dealing with the Gulf war.

<u>Direction of the Story</u>: Defined as the story being critical or non-critical of Saddam Hussein. My use of "direction" should be considered as similar to Lamey's construct of "valence."

<u>Subject Matter of the Story</u>: Classifying subject matter of Gulf war stories into 20 topical categories.

This research counted the frequency of occurrence within each category; percentages are calculated to show the overall distribution. Since no specific hypothesis was tested, no statistical tests were run.

Research Data

The three main aspects of this study -- amount of front page coverage, topics covered, direction of news -- produced detailed compilations of data. For ease of reading and subsequent analysis, Appendix E presents the charted data.

Front page coverage by the newspapers can be considered in three war time periods, early, middle and late. Press studies have illustrated that event coverage has initiation, peak and decline phases. It is not surprising that the Egyptian papers studied exhibited this process. What may be somewhat of a surprise is the degrees to which they responded. An overview of the percentage coverages by paper and time periods makes this clear:

War Time Periods	Al-Ahram	Al-Wafd	Al-Shaab
Early (Jan. 14-22)	87 - 100	80 - 100	48 - 86
Middle (Jan. 23-Feb. 21)	54 - 100	48 - 100	65 - 77
Late (Feb. 22-28)	67 - 100	74 - 100	91.5

The longer middle time period shows a decline of coverage as it possibly became more difficult to maintain high saliency on a daily basis. *Al-Wafd*, in particular, dropped below half of its front page stories reporting the war. *Al-Shaab*, however, exhibited continued coverage increases over the time periods.

The diversity of topics covered during the six weeks of military action also provides coverage detail. The amount and type of coverage is dichotomous in the national and opposition presses. Certain topics covered by the national press were not mentioned by the opposition press, especially *Al-Shaab*. This paper did not report President Mubarak's statements, pro-U.S. positions, official UN statements, pro-peace efforts, rebuilding of Kuwait and progress in peace negotiations.

On the other hand, both *Al-Ahram* and *Al-Wafd* mention those points. Most of the information, apart from President Mubarak's statements, came from international wires and CNN. According to a member of the Editorial Board of *Al-Shaab*, his newspaper never stressed using this presumed biased information. Therefore, if we look at the subjects covered most by *Al-Shaab*, we will find they are opinionated news coverage, much of which was against the U.S. (19.2% of the 52 stories). *Al-Shaab* also used larger stories and therefore their number, even on the front page, was much less than many other papers. The Al-Shaab source added that his paper was not keen on reporting the progress of military actions, as it all came from a source they did not trust. Instead, they reported on January 29 that "it is clear that America failed to achieve its goals; Iraq's resistance is a good sign; it has chances to win the war." On February 12, 1991, *Al-Shaab* quoted Saddam Hussein saying, "Every day that passes is getting us closer to the victory."

If there appeared any uniformity among the presses, it was of the direction of news stories. It is not surprising that they were, overall, negative. Keep in mind that the amount of coverage by *Al-Shaab* was at the minimum, and therefore, is not a representative "negative." The national paper, *Al-Ahram*, was certainly the most "negative," with 295 of 300 stories critical of Saddam.

Conclusion

This unit began with a review of Egyptian press law development to illustrate the presumption that in Egypt there are operating two general models of the press -- those of social responsibility and libertarian. By studying three components of press coverage -- front page news, topic coverage and direction of news -- the generalized nature of press roles and responsibilities are observed. Clearly, *Al-Ahram*, *Al-Wafd* and *Al-Shaab* represent divergent points-of-view and methods. For example, *Al-Ahram* was intensive of its "Mubarak -- pro-US -- peace" coverage. The opposition *Al-Wafd* lightly covered similar issues. Nothing should suggest that they should have done otherwise, if one accepts the contention that Egypt has an open press. In this scenario, even the most stringent opposition press would be pan-Arab and position itself for Arab unity, in opposition to Saddam and the invasion of Kuwait. We assume that the three newspapers studied are representative enough to make that assumption. Another war is not necessary to validate the assumption. Continued research of coverage on other crisis/salient issues for the Egyptian public will establish or deny it.

Political Press Cartoons During the Crisis

Richard Boylan

One often hears that if Egyptians stopped joking and smiling, Egypt is in for a rough time. One, also hears, however, that when Egyptians laugh a lot they know they are in for bad times. Whatever the case, Egyptians take their humor seriously, and in serious times they are said to depend upon a survival mechanism called the *nukta*, the "precursor of the pictorial cartoon in Egypt" (Marsot, 1971, 6).

A *nukta* is a complex joke or satirical story or farce that circulates by word of mouth. And, according to Marsot, "it is in times of crisis that the basic function of the *nukta* appears, that of a safety valve, making people laugh where they would otherwise collapse in despair" (6). For example, one Gulf crisis *nukta* circulating told of the man who asked a college girl to marry him so that she could translate CNN for him. Other stories were often told at the expense of the Upper Egypt Egyptian, or "Saeidy." One, relating to the hardships of the Egyptian working abroad, was told about the Saeidy working in Iraq during the Gulf conflict. When he mentioned to his cousin that he wanted to leave Iraq, his cousin reminded him not to tell the border guards he was Egyptian, because, as they both knew, Iraqis did not like Egyptians. So when he reached the border and was asked his nationality, he answered, "Kuwaiti."

Another good example of a *nukta* was the claim that international policy dictated that Iraq invade Kuwait, and that in turn, Kuwait invade Muhandessin (a section of Cairo overflowing with Kuwaitis during the war).

Cartooning in one form or another may be one of Egypt's oldest forms of expression. Over five thousand years ago Egyptians "presented satirical deformation and comic apologies in sculpture, drama and paintings" (El-Tarabichi, 1975, 25).

Cartooning in Egypt may or may not be as old as hieroglyphics, depending on how cartooning is defined, but Marsot places the start of cartooning in Egypt as late as the end of the nineteenth century. Cartooning began "as an expression of growing feelings of antagonism towards the ruler," (2) by a small group of intellectuals in hopes of moulding public opinion. Since that time, cartooning in Egypt has been progressively popular. (For a thorough discussion of the history of cartooning in Egypt, see El Tarabichi.)

It has been argued that cartooning in Egypt has its own logic based on coping with oppression that separates it from the logic of Western cartooning. Egypt has a history of being oppressed by poverty, disease and foreign rule. Even today, about 50% of Egyptians over ten are functionally illiterate (*Egypt Profiles*, 1991, 10), a condition that depreciates the value of the written word (Marsot, 6). Egypt is no longer under direct foreign rule, but still remains significantly dependent on aid from other nations, and the Egyptian population has lived under emergency laws since Sadat's assassination. The emergency laws "give the police virtually unlimited powers to seize property, break up public gatherings and control the media and printing presses" (*Egypt Profiles*, 1989-90, 6). President Mubarak, however, publicly stands against political repression of the press. As other contributors in this volume note, to what degree the Egyptian press can be said to be free is still lively debated.

Be that as it may, the claim is that humor has historically allowed Egyptians to persevere -- and that the *nukta* and the cartoon have played a role in that perseverance.

The invasion of Kuwait on August 2, 1990, did not create hard times in Egypt, though it may have exacerbated them. The influx of Egyptian workers escaping the threat of hostilities in the Gulf added pressure to an already crowded Cairo. Add to these numbers the refugees from Kuwait and other countries and the corresponding taxing of facilities, and one gets a sense of the condition under which Egyptians and the expatriate community lived and Egyptian press worked.

Egypt's role in the Gulf conflict was central, psychologically, politically, militarily and geographically. While presenting to the world a monolithic stance, Egypt was threatened by terrorism from without and subversion from within. Threats against Egypt were well publicized as were stories of potential uprisings, especially by Muslim fundamentalist factions who would draw support from those Egyptians suffering from the extreme poverty of the country. Reports of unrest in neighboring North African and Middle East states, and the fear that Israel would enter the hostilities, all joined to create a climate of apprehension in Egypt during the period.

Cartooning During The Crisis

If, indeed, cartoons have served as a safety valve in the time of war and oppression, Egyptians had an ample opportunity during the Gulf crisis to find a safety valve furnished by Egyptian newspapers, magazines and cartoon books. There was no shortage of cartoons published during this period. An examination of a sample of these cartoons reveals a variety of themes in a variety of flavors, which, to the extent those themes reflect Egyptian public concerns, gives an impression of the breadth of their concerns. This section seeks to reveal those concerns while including a little of the cartoons' flavor.

During the Gulf war cartoonists characterized an array of domestic, regional and international topics, as well as the events of the Gulf crisis. Cartoonists concerned themselves with a number of themes, among them: the effects of television in general and the impact of CNN in particular; concerns about the environment; the general elections; and world events such as those occurring in the Soviet Union. The impact of the Gulf crisis was related to problems in the Egyptian economy, the collapse of tourism, terrorism and anti-Israel sentiment, problems with Arab unity, military debt, and the fear of the West, particularly the U.S., establishing a foothold in the Middle East. Concern in Egypt over what the new year would bring and the January 15 "war" deadline were also dominant themes.

For this discussion, the majority of cartoons representing those themes were selected from reprints in *The Egyptian Gazette* from *Caricature* Magazine, *Al-Gomhureya, Al Ahram, Sabah El Kheir* Magazine, *Rose El Yousef, Al Messa, Al Akhbar, Al Wafd* (opposition daily), *Al Ahali* (opposition weekly), and *Horreyati* magazine. Additional cartoons were selected directly from Arabic sources and translated. (A more specific analysis of selected cartoons from *Akhbar Al-Yom, Al-Ahram* and *Al-Wafd* is Khalil's (1991) "Cartoon Strips in the Egyptian Press during the Gulf Crisis.")
Among these publications and their cartoonists, styles varied as did themes. Graphically, some efforts appeared more illustrative than attempts at humor, while others approached the raucous, racy and blatant. Single-panel as well as multi-panel cartoons were featured.

Problems at Home and Abroad

The Gulf conflict offered Egyptian cartoonists a plethora of themes to test

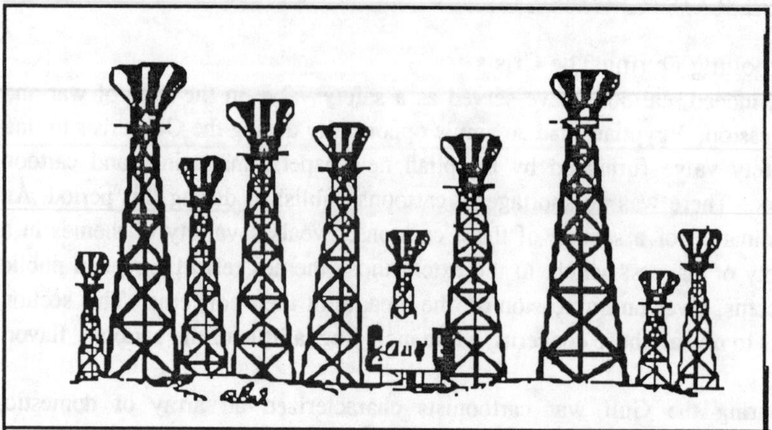

US to maintain permanent token pressence in the Gulf

Gomaa in ROSE EL YOUSSEF

Gomaa in ROSE EL YOUSSEF

their skills, imagination and wit. During the period, a steady flow of cartoons hit the streets. While the Gulf situation clearly dominated the cartoonists' agendas, the cartoons during this period did not exclusively focus on the the Gulf conflict. For example, *Al Ahram* took note through a Dawoud cartoon of Margaret Thatcher's resignation (*Egyptian Gazette*, Nov. 26). Gomma in *Rose El Yousef* showed Gorbachev stepping over a shattered hammer and sickle on his way to accepting the Nobel Peace Prize. (*Egyptian Gazette*, Oct. 22). Amru Selim in *Rose El Yousef* took time to show the what the rule of "Gorby" did to the spelling of "rUSsA" (*Egyptian Gazette*, Dec. 3). Other cartoonists chose to celebrate the introduction of CNN in Egypt by jabbing television from time to time. Sayed Hakem in *Horreyati* magazine (*Egyptian Gazette*, Dec. 10) showed a mother trying to get her son to say "Daddy...Mommy," but he would only say "TV...Video." Farag Hassan in *Al Ahram* showed a woman on the phone saying, "CNN has taken my husband like another woman would," while her husband stares into the television set (Jan. 31). One cartoon by Mustafa Hussein showed a group of men smoking *shiisha* and drinking tea watching CNN. One man is saying, "They can know about everything in the world, but our neighbor had her laundry stolen and they did not mention it on CNN" (*Akhbar al-Yom*, Feb. 2).

The concern about pollution was highlighted in several cartoons, especially on World Anti Pollution Day. Maher Dawoud celebrated the "International Conference in Cairo on the Dangers of Pesticide" by showing the globe, tongue forced out of its mouth by the noose around its neck, hanging from a pesticide can (*Egyptian Gazette*, Dec. 19).

During this period a major election was held in Egypt and cartoonists reacted by harassing the candidates at the same time they were noting the plight of the Egyptian refugees flooding into Egypt from the Gulf region.

On a lighter note, Mustafa Hussein noted the postponement of Love Day festivals with a cartoon showing a husband thanking God for the delay as a rather stout but well endowed wife stands poised (*Egyptian Gazette*, Nov. 5).

The effects of the crisis on the Egyptian economy was most evident in the collapse of tourism in Egypt (*Economist*, 1991, 34). Mohammed Hakem in *Sabah El Kheir* (*Egyptian Gazette*, Nov. 16). characterized the industry's plight by showing a frightened girl, "Tourism," with a noose around her neck, standing on a stool about to have a figure whose arms are labelled "Raising fees to visit tourist sites" and the "Gulf Crisis" pull the stool out from under her (*Egyptian Gazette*, Nov 16). In another cartoon, Hakem depicted

Tourism as a withering flower, no longer receiving water because the knife of the Gulf crisis has cut the garden hose (*Sabah El Kheir* magazine in *Egyptian Gazette*, Dec. 11). Hakem's fears were borne out as tourism fell off to a trickle, causing additional economic hardship for thousands of Egyptians. As these cartoons reveal, there were plenty of problems for the Egyptians to worry about independent of the Gulf situation. But during this period it was difficult to separate out domestic issues from Gulf crisis issues, for the crisis permeated all of Egyptian life. The Gulf crisis gave Egyptians more to worry about at home, on top of those on-going international threats they had lived with for years.

Hostilities and War

Terrorism is always a possibility within Egypt, but during this period overt threats made it highly probable. The possibility of terrorism destabilizing the region was raised by Toghan in *Al-Gomhureya* (*Egyptian Gazette*, Oct. 15), at the same time that the "massacre at the Aqsa Mosque" was depicted by Maher Dawoud in *Al Ahram* (Oct. 15), with Dawoud asking "But, who's the dramatist?" of this "Middle East Tragedy." Gomaa in *Rose Al Yousef* raised the concern that Gulf events would put a noose around the world, restraining its ability to help "Holy Jerusalem" (*Egyptian Gazette*, Oct. 15).

The Israeli threat to the Arab world is a perpetual theme of Egyptian cartoonists. Anti-Israeli cartoons depicted Israeli leaders overseeing a grave which would be "the permanent residents (sic) for the Arabs" (*Egyptian Gazette*, Oct. 29). Mohamed Hakem in *Al Ahali*, an opposition weekly, drew a faltering Arab with an Israeli dagger in his back and a ball and chain labelled "Gulf Crisis" around one foot and a ball and chain around his wrist labelled "Arab division" (*Egyptian Gazette*, Jan. 13).

The issue of Arab unity was treated by several cartoonists. The Arab nations, symbolized in the form of a man who is attempting to block four cannons, one limb to each muzzle, depicts the Arab nation as being pulled apart by hostilities (Nagi in *Al Ahram*, Oct. 15). Amru Selim made the suggestion that the West might want to see the Arab nations fight each other when he drew two Arabs facing off with rifles aimed at the other but with barrels bent towards themselves as a gleeful Western man looked on (*Rose El Yousef*, in *Egyptian Gazette*, Nov. 26).

The fear of large military debts and the prospect of paying the United

Mohamed Hakem in *Sabah el Kheir magazine*

Mahar Dawoud in *AL AHRAM*

States for the cost of the war were featured by Farag Hassan in *Al Ahram* and Bahgat in *Al Ahali* (*Egyptian Gazette*, Nov. 19). Mohamed Hakem in *Al Ahali* (opposition weekly) had a poor, tattered boy asking a U.S. soldier to "Please give me some of the money you pay for a missile to buy food!" (*Egyptian Gazette*, Feb. 18). Gomaa in *Rose El Yousef* proclaimed "The devastating impact of Iraqi Invasion on the Arab region" by showing Uncle Sam "sticking up" an Arab sheikh who is standing by his open safe with his hands up (*Egyptian Gazette*, Feb. 20).

The cartoon of George Bush watering a well-armed soldier who has already sprouted roots in an area designated Gulf needs no words to express the regional concern that the Gulf conflict was a pretext for the West to establish a permanent force in the Gulf region. (*Rose El Yousef*, in *Egyptian Gazette*, Nov. 19)

With the coming of the new year and the January 15 deadline set by coalition forces for Saddam to leave Kuwait, Egyptian cartoonists turned to the public's fears and uncertainties as to what 1991 would bring. Many cartoonists saw January 15 as the real New Year's day. Farag Hassan in *Al Ahram* showed an old, dishevelled 1990 saying to shapely 1991, "You must know I'll stay on until January 15." As the deadline approached, Mustafa Hussein in *Al Akhbar* had a New Year's man, gas mask in hand, say on the telephone (as a gas-masked person stands in the background), "I'm not going out for the New Years' Eve. I'll spend the Jan. 15 eve at home!" (*Egyptian Gazette*, Jan. 15).

Several cartoonists used a bomb with lit fuse to show the mood of the times as the new year and the impending war approached. Mohamed Hakem in *Al Ahali* had a Father Time/Santa Claus figure handing a youth a lit bomb wrapped in ribbon (*Egyptian Gazette*, Jan. 3). Rauf in *Sabah El-Kheir* has the world sitting worrying beside a Christmas tree with lit bombs underneath as packages (*Egyptian Gazette*, Jan. 3). And as 1990 says to a primping 1991, "I was as young and pretty as you until I turned old on August 2." (Maher Dawoud, in *Al Ahram, Egyptian Gazette*, Jan. 3).

The uncertainties of the period were repeatedly addressed in the Cairo papers and magazines. Tag in *Al Messa* and Nagi and Dawoud in *Al Ahram* employed the warrior Mars to raise the question, Will it be war or peace? Dawoud had Mars juggling angels holding olive branches. Tag asked, "Who will climb?" the ladder to "Tuesday, January 15," Mars or the goddess of peace? And Nagi had Mars having his fortune told (*Egyptian Gazette*, Jan.

15). The world appears to be plucking leaves off an olive branch in a "she loves me, she loves me not" fashion but instead it's, "War....destruction....war... destruction" in Maher Dawoud's (*Al Ahram, Egyptian Gazette*, Jan. 17) cartoon.

Not all the wartime cartoons were that serious. Maher Dawoud in *Al Ahram* had a man and a woman sitting on a park bench rubbing the noses of their gas masks as hearts float above (*Egyptian Gazette*, Feb. 18).

Regional politics related to the war's outcome was also a dominant theme. Mohsen had a man reading about the Gulf war from a newspaper asking another man, "Will Israel remain so well behaved?" (*Egyptian Gazette*, March 4). Gomaa in *Rose El Yousef* had Uncle Sam hauling in Iraq in a fish net while Rafsanjani of Iran and Ozal of Turkey stand by, fishing poles in hand (*Egyptian Gazette*, March 12).

Several Egyptian cartoonists were particularly adept at caricaturing international leaders like Rafsanjani and Ozal. Uncle Sam, Gorbachev, King Hussein, Yasser Arafat, Arab sheiks, Yitzhak Shamir, and George Bush were favorite subjects. However, generally absent from the flow of Gulf crisis cartoons in the Egyptian national press were caricatures of Egyptian leaders, most notably Hosni Mubarak. With a few exceptions published in the opposition press, cartoonists looked elsewhere for their targets, and more than likely their primary target was Saddam Hussein.

Ridiculing Saddam

Absent from cartoons about the Iraqi president was Iraq itself and the Iraqi people. It was Saddam's war. Saddam was seen as the instigator and the combatant. Rather than "demonizing' Saddam as George Bush and American television did (Liebs 1992, 52), Egyptian cartoonists treated Saddam more as a spoiled child and an idiot. Saddam was a comic character, as was King Hussein, Yasser Arafat and, to some extent, George Bush. Hussein and Arafat were portrayed as toadies, lackeys and dupes. On the other hand, Israel and its leaders were portrayed as strictly demonic. Saddam was mocked, Israeli leaders were reviled.

Egyptian editorial cartoonists delighted in ridiculing Saddam. Marsot asserts that "ridicule is a deadly weapon," especially "to people who are as conscious of 'face' as Easterners are" (Marsot, 4). Whether this be the case, from the invasion on, and from all quarters of the Egyptian cartooning press,

Amru Selim in Rose El Youss

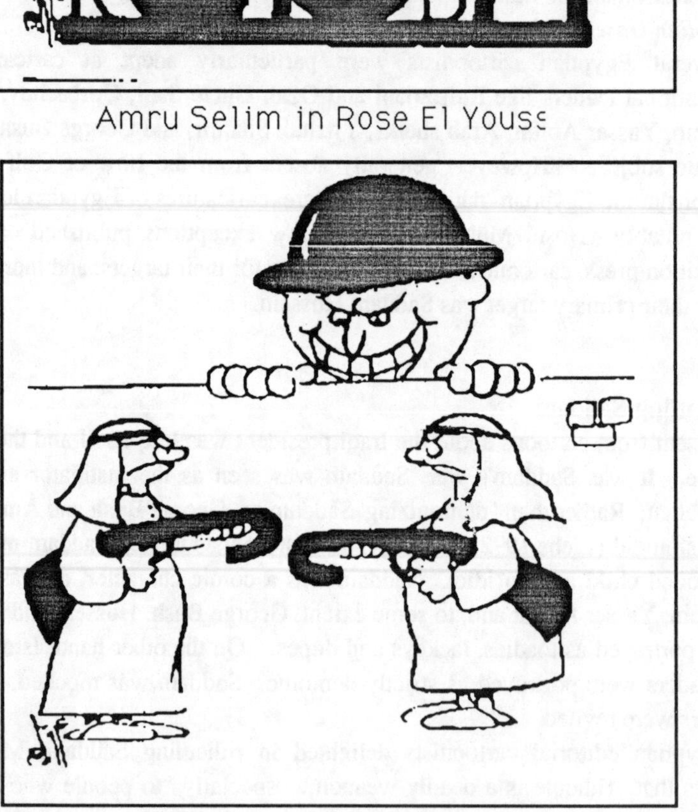

Amru Selim in Rose El Youss

Saddam was subjected to this most "deadly weapon" of ridicule and a strong measure of mockery.

Mustafa Hussein researched Saddam's childhood and reported in the "Childhood Story of Saddam," a three-panel cartoon, that Saddam was born with a moustache (a manly feature), and that he was the talk of all Baghdad when the nurse found a grenade in his diaper. The last frame claims that at six months the little moustachioed Saddam was asked what he wanted to eat, and he answered, "Kuwait!" (*Akhbar al-Yom*, Feb. 16).

Before the coalition forces' attack, Gomaa in *Rose El Yousef* showed a haggard, startled Saddam jumping back after he has opened an oil barrel releasing a jack-in-the-box Uncle Sam. (*Egyptian Gazette*, Oct. 8) In December, Maher Dawoud in *Al Ahram* (*Egyptian Gazette*, Dec. 13) depicted a small Saddam in a mouse cage being examined by George Bush who has a flashlight labelled "Bush overture" and holds a "U.N." club in his right hand. Also, in December, Gomaa in *Rose El Yousef* was warning Saddam he had miscalculated. He depicted Saddam charging toward Kuwait's oil fields, sword raised and calculating in his head, "2+2=6, 4+1=7, 3+3=2, 5+6=13" (*Egyptian Gazette*, Dec. 31) .

Mustafa Hussein in *Al Akhbar* showed a pensive Saddam looking into a mirror asking, "Will it be war or not, are you nuts?" (*Egyptian Gazette*, Jan. 17). Meanwhile, Toghan in *Al-Gomhureya* had Saddam jumping on an island Kuwait trying to evade two leaping sharks, one called "invasion" and the other called "withdrawal" (*Egyptian Gazette*, Jan. 15).

Mustafa Hussein, perhaps Saddam's greatest cartoon nemesis, attacked Saddam in the press and in his own "Saddam" cartoon book published during the crisis. In a stream of cartoons, Saddam was skewered on Hussein's pen. He showed Iraqi soldiers surrendering in the face of the U.S.'s greatest weapon, the hamburger (Feb. 26). In another panel Hussein showed two Iraqis in a dugout saying, "We can't give up now and go back. Americans will soon come with hamburgers" (*Akhbar al-Yom*, Feb. 27).

Hussein featured King Hussein of Jordan as a little windup toy speaking into a microphone under Saddam's control. Saddam is saying to a subordinate, "No, his highness's speech is a good one, but I have to push him for more rude words" (*Akhbar al-Yom*, Feb. 14). King Hussein remained the butt of the joke in another panel in which Saddam is carrying the tiny King, who is saying, "You know Saddam, I have never been that tall except when I'm beside you" (*Akhbar al-Yom.*, Feb. 13). Hussein showed a beaten

Saddam sitting exhausted on a chair and King Hussein and Yasser Arafat stealing off. The king is saying, "Excuse me, I need to go pray in Amman." Arafat is saying, "Excuse me, also. I need to go to the toilet in Tunisia, then I'll be back soon." When Tariq Aziz gives Saddam the V sign with his two fingers, Saddam asks, "Do you mean we have won the war?" Aziz responds, "No, I mean there are just two of us left" (Mustafa Hussein, *Akhbar al-Yom*, Feb. 24). In another three-panel cartoon Hussein tells us that Saddam contemplated suicide. In the second frame he decides he will have Aziz kill him. In the third frame he asks Aziz, "Are you going to kill me?" In the fourth frame Saddam has shot Aziz.

The ridicule of Saddam continued from both the government press and the opposition press right up to the cease fire. Abdul Helim showed a tattered Saddam pulling a burned-out tank on a string (*Egyptian Gazette*, March 4). Nagi in *Al Ahram* had Saddam giving the V for victory as he holds a pistol to his head (*Egyptian Gazette*, March 4). Gomaa in *Al Wafd* (opposition daily) had two men observing a Saddam with a huge tongue wagging in front of his face saying, "The most feared leader has lost all his army. So what? What matters is that he still has his most effective weapon!" obviously referring to his wagging tongue (*Egyptian Gazette*, March 4).

Nagi in *Al Ahram* showed Saddam tied in knots asking, "But who will set me free?" (*Egyptian Gazette*, March 12). A weeping Saddam kneeling at the feet of a seated skeleton holding a Scythe was done by Maher Dawoud in *Al Ahram*. Saddam is crying that the reconstruction of Kuwait will ruin all his good works (*Egyptian Gazette*, March 31).

But perhaps the most prophetic of the cartoons of this period was Mustafa Hussein's four panel discussion between Tariq Aziz and Saddam. The question is, where will Saddam escape to? Will it be Moscow? Aziz asks. No, Saddam says, I don't like Moscow. Will it be Algeria? No, I don't like Algeria. Will it be India? No, I don't like India. So, says Tariq, where do you prefer? To which Saddam answers, "I still love Kuwait!"

Conclusion

Throughout this volume analyses have looked at various aspects of newspaper content. What has been made clear is that there were, in fact, primary differences between national and opposition presses' amounts and types of coverage and the attitude valences they held. At times the implication of the authors is that the Egyptian press held back from dynamic, assertive coverage. It is even suggested that the journalists often had little understanding of the extent to which their stories could go. As should be evident from this unit, that certainly was not the case with Egypt's cartoonists in the gulf crisis and the pens they loosed.

If, as Marsot said, "The function of any cartoon is to influence the spectator for or against something, either by presenting it as a figure worthy of sympathy, or by distorting it into a figure of ridicule" (2), then clearly the Egyptian cartoonist took a staunch stand against Saddam and his deeds. Again, though even as a cursory comparison, cartoons jumped in where independent, non-wire-service print journalism from Egypt dared not go. Even the extremist opposition *Al-Shaab* gingered about when being anti-U.S.

Whether cartoons served as a safety valve for an oppressed Egyptian population is a topic for future investigators. Socio-political research questions about Arab sister states having direct confrontation in print versus cartoon form could possibly provide additional "coverage" insight. The final salvo of cartooning may be that ridiculing the enemy could make him appear less formidable. Were that truly the case, then based on the treatment and extent of Egyptian editorial cartooning during the crisis, Saddam should have been rendered impotent.

Assessments of Gulf Crisis Photojournalism Coverage

Hussein Amin

Photojournalism is one of the most important aspects of journalism. Pictures and words together have a more powerful impact than each of them can have alone (Shuneman, 1972). Photographic communication has emerged in recent decades as an essential mode of mass communication (Agee et al., 1988). Since the visual dimension is capable of bypassing illiteracy, it can provide a wealth of description and detail of events not communicable through the written or spoken word.

The power of pictures to influence reader perception was extensively studied by Miller (1975). Miller claimed that photographs are among the first news items to catch the reader's eye, and they usually assist in establishing the context or frame of reference in which the reader interprets an accompanying story. Woodburn (1983) reported that photos are the only representations of world events. Whatever the subject of the photograph, the pictures take on an additional quality when the photo editor places them to form an eye-catching, compelling photo-story or to remain separate units to co-exist with the picture (Kobre, 1980). These elements make the pictures in newspapers potentially important conveyors of information (Lester et al., 1990).

Photojournalism is particularly important when it concerns page one of a newspaper. There are two reasons why we should consider page one to be of interest. First, it helps the the paper to sell when displayed on news stands. Second, it helps to get the whole paper read. "If the purchaser glances over the front page headlines and big stories then throws it away, the advertisers will not be getting results and will therefore not advertise again in that paper" (Vitray et al., 1932). And, of course, in times of crises such as war, readers may be drawn to copy content by page one photo stimulation.

The problem lies in the fact that Egyptian newspapers do not seem to include diverse and relevant photojournalistic material on their front pages, in spite of its obvious importance in arousing readers' interest and therefore increasing the paper's dissemination.

Research Question and Method

This research examined and evaluated photojournalism in Egypt during the gulf crisis using content analysis of the front page photos in four major Egyptian newspapers (pro-government and opposition).

Three research questions were asked: 1) Was photojournalism correctly used in the Egyptian newspapers; 2) Did opposition newspapers use more or more effective photos than the national newspapers; and 3) Did political point-of-view affect the selection of front-page photos?

The data for this study consisted of photographs that appeared on the front pages of national and opposition newspapers during the gulf crisis. Four leading newspapers were chosen because of their national prominence and large circulations. They were *Al-Akhbar* (daily, pro-government), *Al-Ahram* (daily, pro-government), *Al-Wafd* (daily, opposition) and *Al-Ahali* (weekly, opposition).

Al-Akhbar and *Al-Ahram* represent the official government line (in spite of the occasional criticisms which appear either in the editorials or "Letters to the Editor" sections). In addition, their circulation is wider than any other national (pro-government) paper such as *Missa* or *Al-Gomhureya* newspapers.

Al-Wafd and *Al-Ahali* were chosen for similar reasons. They are the two leading symbols of Egypt's political opposition. They represent, respectively, the Neo-Wafdist party and the National Progressive Union Party (NPUP).

Six issues of each newspaper were selected for a sample of twenty-four issues. It was concluded from a preliminary analysis that fewer issues would not be fair representation of each newspaper's coverage in this duration of time. Different pictures of the war and related matters are scattered among many issues of each paper throughout the year. Clustering of significant news events within a specific time span was important as it would minimize the risk of missing important instances of war coverage. This study covered two main time phases:

Phase I: The airstrike phase, lasting from the start of hostilities on January 16 to the declaration of the ground attack on February 26, 1990.

Phase II: The ground attack phase, reported in the February 26, 1990, issues (this is represented in the research by only one issue of each of the four papers).

Photo data were submitted to an expert panel to make judgments of the photos using a pass/fail technique. All experts had practical or theoretical photography experience and have published research and other writings on related topics.

Limitations of the Study

A decision was made to limit the size of the study to the front page of each issue owing to the relative importance of this page, as previously mentioned. The gulf crisis period was focused on because it had been the most sensational and attention-getting recent event.

The data were collected, scored, and analyzed in terms of both picture and caption on the following points:

1. Placement of the photo on the page
2. Size of the photo in relation to text
3. Content of the photo in relation to the gulf crisis
4. Relation of the photo to the text
5. Caption and its relation to photo and text
6. Impact of the political perspective of the newspaper on the photo.

Panelists used a system of "pass" for photographs meeting each criteria and "fail" when photographs did not meet the criteria.

Results

Figures 5 to 8 report the expert panel judgments of the newspaper issues according to the evaluation criteria.

Out of the total number of pages studied from all of the newspapers during the period of the gulf crisis, 54% contained a photograph. This percentage is divided between national newspapers (29%) and opposition newspapers (25%). Of all the examined pictures, 58% had a good size in relation to the text. This percentage is split between national and opposition newspapers where the share of national newspaper was 25% and the opposition newspapers' share was 29%. This result answers the first research question by suggesting that photojournalism was incorrectly used in Egyptian

Fig. 5 Al-Akhbar - Analysis of Gulf War Photos on the Front Page

Category / Date	Place of photo	Size in relation to text	Content in relation to crisis	Relation to text	Relation of caption to photo and text	Impact in relation to political perspective
Jan. 17, 1991	P	P	P	F	P	F
Jan. 25, 1991	P	P	P	P	P	P
Feb. 1, 1991	P	F	F	P	F	F
Feb. 8, 1991	F	F	F	F	F	F
Feb. 18, 1991	F	P	P	P	F	P
Feb. 26, 1991	F	P	P	P	P	P

P = "pass", F = "fail" in terms of the evaluation criteria.

Fig. 6 Al-Ahram - Analysis of Gulf War Photos on the Front Page

Category / Date	Place of photo	Size in relation to text	Content in relation to crisis	Relation to text	Relation of caption to photo and text	Impact in relation to political perspective
Jan. 17, 1991	F	F	F	F	F	F
Jan. 25, 1991	P	P	F	P	P	F
Feb. 1, 1991	F	P	P	P	F	P
Feb. 8, 1991	F	F	F	F	F	F
Feb. 18, 1991	F	F	F	F	F	P
Feb. 26, 1991	P	P	P	P	P	P

P = "pass", F = "fail" in terms of the evaluation criteria.

Fig. 7 **Al-Wafd - Analysis of Gulf War Photos on the Front Page**

Category / Date	Place of photo	Size in relation to text	Content in relation to crisis	Relation to text	Relation of caption to photo and text	Impact in relation to political perspective
Jan. 17, 1991	F	F	F	F	F	F
Jan. 25, 1991	P	P	F	P	P	P
Feb. 1, 1991	F	F	F	F	F	F
Feb. 8, 1991	P	P	F	P	F	P
Feb. 18, 1991	P	P	P	P	F	P
Feb. 26, 1991	P	P	P	P	P	P

P = "pass", F = "fail" in terms of the evaluation criteria.

Fig. 8 Al-Ahaly - Analysis of Gulf War Photos on the Front Page

Category / Date	Place of photo	Size in relation to text	Content in relation to crisis	Relation to text	Relation of caption to photo and text	Impact in relation to political perspective
Jan. 17, 1991	P	P	P	P	F	F
Jan. 25, 1991	P	F	F	F	P	P
Feb. 1, 1991	F	F	F	F	F	F
Feb. 8, 1991	P	F	F	F	F	F
Feb. 18, 1991	P	P	F	P	F	P
Feb. 26, 1991	P	P	P	P	F	P

P = "pass", F = "fail" in terms of the evaluation criteria.

The data also indicated that 58.3% of all newspaper photos studied had good relation to the text. Of this total, the share for national newspapers was 29.2% and for opposition newspapers 29.1%. These results reinforce the answer to the second question, that opposition and national papers were equally ineffective in photo use.

Data suggest that for national and opposition newspapers the relationship between caption and photograph, as well as text, was not clearly identified. Of all pictures placed on the front pages in national and opposition newspapers, only 33.3% indicated caption relation to photos and text. National newspapers' share in this category was 20.8%. Opposition newspapers' share was 12.5%.

In the final category, political point-of-views affect photo selection, data suggest it may have had an impact. In 50% of the selected national and opposition newspapers, the political point-of-view of the paper had an impact on the kinds of photographs displayed in the front pages. Both national and opposition newspapers had a share of 25%.

Discussion

After reviewing the results of this study, the author contends that Egyptian newspapers do not consider photojournalism an important form of journalism. In view of the historical importance, regional significance, and strong public interest in the Gulf war, the data should have reflected greater and more appropriate use of photos. The fact that they did not is in itself revealing. During a national and regional crisis, both pro-government and opposition newspapers continued to downplay photojournalism.

The Egyptian print media clearly had little regard for photojournalism and the possibilities it offers. The newspapers examined in this study tended to under-utilize pictures of the crisis. In not one case did any of the pro-government or opposition newspapers display their own photographs of the gulf crisis, relying completely on other sources, such as photo agencies or CNN photo "stills."

While these newspapers currently use photojournalism to some degree, the level is far below that of most newspapers in the developed world. This under-utilization is due to several factors, particularly the lack of a truly competitive market. National newspapers are not concerned about their circulation since they are subsidized by the government; there is, therefore, little incentive to increase circulation. On the other hand, opposition newspapers face severe financial difficulties and, therefore, cannot afford field correspondents.

In order to develop and improve the use of photojournalism in Egypt, publishers, editors, reporters, and photographers must increase their awareness of the potential of photojournalism and be encouraged to redouble their efforts to improve its utilization in Egypt.

Global Media:
Looking In -- Looking Out

CNN: News, War, and Government Control
Ted Turner

What my philosophy has been for CNN since the very beginning, is that number one, we will tell the truth as close as we can find it on controversial issues and then let the viewers, wherever they are located, draw their own conclusions.

This is, I feel, a big difference about the way NBC, CBS and ABC used to do things. I remember, for instance, when the President would speak to the American people back in the old days, the second it was done with, the cameras went straight to Walter Cronkite, who said, "I am going to interpret for you what the president said." Well, I consider that highly insulting because I didn't elect Walter Cronkite as President of the United States. I like Walter Cronkite. I think all the anchors on the television networks are very personable, attractive, highly paid, and intelligent people. But I don't want them interpreting what our political leaders say or what anyone else is saying. I would rather interpret it myself. And what they would do is bend it around to what they believe. In other words, they would be interpreting for you what they personally believe.

And that was one of the reasons I got mad enough to try and do CNN, because I considered it an insult to my intelligence. I didn't want TV people giving their opinions about things because, in all fairness, TV anchors mainly just read TelePrompTers; they don't even write their own copy in some cases. That is why we have ordered the anchor people at CNN not to give their personal opinions about things. Every now and then it does happen because people are only human, and when they are not on the TelePrompTer they sometimes forget. But it is very rare that it happens and it is expressly forbidden. When we want opinions we will go to people who are qualified, widely recognized in their field to make those opinions.

Once CNN got underway and I realized that people in Central South America were seeing the signal, and particularly leadership people, I then realized that we had something that could be valuable to the whole world. We expanded to the whole world and now you can pick up CNN, if you have the right kind of satellite dish, virtually anywhere on the planet, except Poland. We have moved it to be more of an international focus and less the U.S. focus.

Remember, we basically started out with the idea that we are going to stick to the facts and the truth. Censorship and the controlling of news during the gulf conflict was not the first time it was that way. In Granada there was a total blackout of the media and a partial one during the Panama invasion. I am not a journalist or a news person but, as I understand it, there is a real debate going on within the media about what's right for the government to do in so far as controlling the media during wartime. The Iraqi war was the most recent one, but the question still is, what should we, the press, be allowed to see and what should we be kept away from? The honest truth is that I don't have all the answers to that. There are so many media outlets in the United States now and so many of them want to have their own reporters present, that if you gave unlimited access to the media there would probably be more media people on the battlefield than there would be soldiers. The government has a point that access has to be controlled because they can't have hundreds of TV, radio and newspaper journalists running around on the battlefield.

Ed Turner, Executive Vice President of CNN, gave this overview of our position regarding the government's stance and how our broadcasting interfaced with that position.

> War is the public's business. The citizens of America supply the soldiers, the money, and the will to fight. We are strong enough and sophisticated enough to see and hear how our national policy is implemented. The First Amendment part of the Bill of Rights now is two hundred years old and it guarantees this. But as many other guarantees in life, they can be ignored.
>
> For example, we have yet to see the ground war from the Persian

Gulf. The only broadcast of the air war was from the bomb sight cameras of the fighter bombers of the Allies; except when CNN cameras in Baghdad brought the pictures of the bombings; except when our open microphone from the capital of Iraq described the opening of the air war. The coalition governments -- notably the Pentagon -- partly controlled access to its armies, not because the media had released the war plan. CNN, for example, knew of the 7th Corps (the Hail Mary maneuver) several weeks before its execution. So did other news organizations, and we did not report it.

The American public seemed to agree with our reports. In every poll taken by the Times-Mirror foundation during the weeks of bombing, CNN rated ahead of its broadcast competition by numbers ranging from 50% to 60%, to 16% for our closest competitor. At the conclusion of the war, *Newsweek* reported that viewers supported an independent media by a 3:1 margin. The public said it did not want cheerleaders; it wanted its news of the war straight, which brings us back to the First Amendment. Ask the people of Eastern Europe, ask the people of the Baltics and the Soviet Union which kind of government and rights they prefer: A free press or a controlled one? Their answer came in the streets at the barricades, sometimes with their lives.

Constitutionally, I asked CNN's David Collier to view the issue and the summation of his brief is: First, though there is a long history of press coverage of war going back to the Civil War, it's unlikely that the U.S. Supreme Court would mandate the military to provide access. But if the press already had military information in hand, the high court would be more protective of our rights to publish or broadcast, with limitations. They may repress our right to present what is considered to be sensitive military information. The Pentagon papers, for example, may have embarrassed, but did not reveal ongoing operations. This is consistent with CNN policy and the practice of major media, but we do insist on being there.

In the Gulf the Pentagon began with eight camera reporter pools and ended with twenty-eight. These were tightly controlled, and given similar restraints. Ernie Pyle, the W.W. II press correspondent, would have quit. If the Department of Defense had controlled London during the Blitz, Ed Murrow would have been silent.

Recently, television news directors had their convention in Denver. *Broadcasting* magazine commented on the convention issues:

> It has been several months since the end of the Persian Gulf war, but the issue of government censorship during the conflict continued to be a concern among journalists gathered at the Radio and Television News Directors' Association convention. In his annual report to the association's members RTNDA president, David Bartlet, called upon the assembled news directors to stand up for the First Amendment Rights in the face of military restrictions against the press....
>
> At a panel session on the topic, CNN primary anchor, Bernard Shaw, said the conflict between the military and the press during wartime is never going to be resolved. "If you want to control information you control the journalists," said Shaw. "That's why this problem is never going to go away." Nevertheless, efforts are currently underway between the nation's top media organizations and the Defense Department to attempt to resolve the problem of censorship in future conflicts.
>
> Deborah Amos* (here today) said: The relationship between the military and the press in future conflicts will likely be a "more adversarial relationship then we've ever seen" ("Journalists," 1991,28).

I really don't know much more than that.

* Deborah Amos was a presenter at the Ted Turner Symposium on Media and Social Responsibilities. She is a foreign correspondent for National Public Radio, News Division, and covered Desert Storm from a Saudi Arabia location.

Crises and Mass Communication: Lessons of the Gulf War

John Tusa

The experience of broadcasting during the Gulf war set the World Service as a whole, and the BBC Arabic Service in particular, one of the most severe editorial challenges of their existence. As the gulf crisis developed, there was one overriding concern for BBC: to manage and supervise the editorial output so securely that nobody would be able to prove the charge that either the language broadcast was deviating from BBC editorial standards, or that anything other than consistent, balanced and unbiased coverage was broadcast.

It was with that sense of foreboding and realism that BBC faced the early days of the crisis when Iraqi forces invaded Kuwait. The World Service's response was complex, consumed large quantities of management time, and required considerable internal coordination.

This essay addresses gulf crisis BBC coverage in four sections: how BBC changed the broadcasts to meet the demand of events; how many people listened to those broadcasts; how the World Service responded to external criticism of the broadcasts; and finally what conclusions can be drawn about BBC's journalistic response.

From the moment that the Iraqi invasion occurred, it was evident that a swift broadcasting response was needed. Whatever might happen subsequently, the invasion altered the world. Within hours of the invasion on August 2, 1990, BBC increased the broadcasts of the Arabic Service from the existing nine hours to ten and a half. Later they were extended still further to fourteen hours a day. Within 24 hours of the Iraqi attack, jamming of the Arabic Service was observed. It was of the characteristic "wobble type" modulation used by Iraq when it had jammed the BBC and other broadcasts during the Iran-Iraq war, as soon as the U.S. news correspondent broadcast reports of Iraq's use of chemical weapons.

The jamming site was tentatively located as being close to Baghdad, to the south-east of the city. By August 8, it was decided to swamp the jamming by increasing the numbers of frequencies used by the BBC Arabic Service. Accordingly, World Service planners and engineers deployed spare transmitter and frequency time to virtually double the Arabic signal -- expanding from four to seven frequencies in the morning, and from six to eleven in the peak evening listening time. The tactic was successful. The higher frequencies were particularly difficult to jam and after some nine weeks, the jamming stopped altogether, possibly because of the cost of the electricity needed to power it.

The immediate response went beyond the Arabic Service. Many listeners to the World Service in English lived or worked in the Gulf and Middle East. Usually World Service does not target its programs to that area in the night hours because the audience is asleep and it would be a huge waste of electricity. In such crisis conditions, it was felt wrong to deny listeners access to news programs at any time of day or night. World Service (English) on both short and medium wave was put onto a 24-hour transmission pattern to the Middle East from the night of August 8th - 9th.

But listening to Iraq was almost as vital as broadcasting to the area. At BBC Monitoring at Caversham Park, near Reading, where international broadcasts are monitored for news and official statements, two extra staff were allocated to cover broadcasts from the gulf. Further monitoring effort was directed at Iraq to make sure that none of Saddam Hussein's statements would be overlooked.

But at a time of such crisis, BBC was aware that it must use the airwaves to talk very directly to the tens of thousands of third party nationals marooned, threatened, jobless, or, as in the case of American and British citizens in Iraq, detained against their will by Saddam Hussein. For the latter, "Gulf Link," a program of special and personal messages from family and friends to their relatives held hostage in Iraq or Kuwait, was devised. Starting at fifteen minutes a day, it rapidly grew to half an hour per day, transmitted on one special frequency at 1645 hours GMT, expanding to forty-five minutes on three frequencies. It forged a strong bond between the divided families and was often intensely moving to listen to. Those in Britain soon got into the habit of regularly delivering their messages on tape for broadcast; the hostages themselves grew devoted to the presenters of the program.

The plight of the tens of thousands of migrant workers in the gulf from Asian nationalities was also not ignored. Existing broadcasts in Hindu, Urdu,

Pashte and Persian were easily heard in the gulf area as a matter of course. Knowing of the beleaguered existence of thousands of Thais, Bengalis and Indonesians in the Gulf, we allocated each of these 3 services an extra frequency so that they too could be heard by their nationals stuck in the turmoil of the crisis. This action not only earned the gratitude of the governments concerned, but that of the listeners too.

The World Service Audience

Yet anecdotes and thousands of letters remain only that; individual reactions are only valid in their own broad opinion. It was essential to acquire measured assessment of the audience size and its behavior. The received wisdom in the World Service has always been that listening increases sharply during a crisis. Yet it remained only an educated guess, not yet backed with evidence. During the gulf crisis BBC affected a wide geographical area; many parts of it were open to research. That research was conducted in various different states and at different stages of the crisis. The results were revealing and remarkably consistent.

We have three pieces of market research to give us an idea of the extent of listening, conducted at three distinct periods of the crisis. By the end of August 1990, we had completed a survey in the United Arab Emirates, Riyadh, Cairo and Alexandria. The figures for Cairo and Alexandria were typical of those for the entire survey. Before the crisis, 18% of the audience listened to BBC World Service at least once a week. After the crisis, the figure rose almost three-fold to 46%. In addition, 28% said they had listened "yesterday," confirming the picture of serious and regular listening. The BBC emerged as the most listened-to foreign broadcaster, ahead of Saudi Radio and the commercial Radio Monte Carlo.

How important was the BBC as a news source at the start of the crisis? Six percent of the sample in Cairo and Alexandria said they first heard of the invasion of Kuwait from the BBC World Service. But 37% turned to us for confirmation of the event and/or for further information. Those who mentioned radio in general as a source for news in Cairo and Alexandria were 75%, against 74% who mentioned television, and 25% who said they turned to newsprint.

In Cairo and Alexandria, 91% of our audience listened in Arabic, the remaining 9% in English. The pattern in Riyadh and the Emirates was very similar -- a large leap in listening to us as the crisis began; and subsequent heavy use of the BBC as a confirmatory source or one for further information.

Four months into the crisis, in November, further research was conducted in the Jordanian capital, Amman. It showed that our weekly audience was 43% of the total. This gave us a listenership twice as large as Radio Monte Carlo, and four times as large as the Voice of America. Eighty-two percent of the audience cited radio as their principal source of news, while 73% mentioned TV. Once people first heard of the crisis, 28% said they turned to the BBC World Service for more news about it.

Further research was conducted in Amman in May 1991, two months after the Gulf war had left the headlines. While the "crisis" listening figures to the BBC had fallen to a regular audience of 27%, this still left the Arabic Service well ahead of its international competitors -- mainly around 10% -- and just ahead of the populist competitor, Radio Monte Carlo. This further research therefore established two facts: first, the strong position of the Arabic Service under "normal" circumstances, and, second, its even greater strength during a crisis even among listeners in a country which often disapproved of the news they felt they were getting from the BBC.

The final piece in this intensive survey of crisis listening in the Middle East came from Syria in February 1991. At 15.6% of the audience in Damascus and Aleppo, the BBC was the second largest foreign broadcaster, second only to Radio Monte Carlo. The daily audience was four times as large as that for the Voice of America. But among BBC listeners, the patterns of tuning in were intensive -- 79% of the BBC's audience said they had tuned in the day before they were interviewed, an unusually high figure.

Finally, there was a qualitative indicator. In the Amman research, as well as that in the Syrian cities, the listeners were asked to score BBC news coverage on a scale from zero to 5. In Amman, BBC scored 3.25, but in Damascus and Aleppo the figure was notably higher at 4.07.

The conclusions from this most detailed set of surveys of listening during a crisis were encouraging. First, they confirmed that the audience did indeed grow dramatically at such times of acute information need. It also grew for reasons consistent with the World Service's aims and purposes. Listeners expected reliability, constancy and authority and voted for BBC favorably with their radio set tuning knobs. Secondly, it reminded those who think of television as the only mass medium, that when it comes to international news, radio plays as large a part in informing the public as does television. Thirdly, it spoke well of BBC's standing *vis-a-vis* its main rivals and competitors. Fourthly, it raised searching questions about the correct way of measuring the audience for international broadcasting.

The standard definition of "a listener" is a person who listens "regularly at least once a week." Yet if international radio is distinctively a communicator at times of need, those who find it essential, indeed life-saving, at such times, must surely count as part of the audience just as much as those who happen to listen regularly. If the broadcasts are to be effective when the need arises -- almost always suddenly and without warning -- then that is a powerful message to the broadcasters; they must be present even when they may not always be much listened to. But the message to researchers is that the yardstick of measurement must include those who use the service only occasionally. The listener in a crisis is as much a valued and significant listener as the regular patron. So far, audience measurements have not adapted to take account of this new perception.

Assessing BBC Integrity

But the generally reassuring and supporting message from the audience research and the listeners' correspondence did not end the matter. With so much at stake for governments as well as people, it was only to be expected that governments would listen closely, and that they would have a view about what they heard. Some Arab governments did not like what they heard and complained to the British government and to the BBC about it. The only correct and prudent response was to demonstrate that the criticisms were being taken seriously, that they would be investigated, that changes would be made if any criticisms proved accurate or well founded, and that detailed monitoring of Arabic Service output was being undertaken.

Retrospective analysis was carried out. BBC made weekly tallies of current affairs items, analyzed by subject matter, dateline, origin and nationality of the speaker. Over several weeks this review demonstrated that BBC had not -- as was alleged -- given more reports from Baghdad than from the alliance countries, or that there were more Iraqi spokesmen heard in voice than those from the alliance. During these reviews, BBC did point out to critics that if the news had been covered by more Western journalists working from Iraq, the tallies might, rightly, have shown a different result. BBC also pointed out to Saudis and Gulfis that if their Ministers were heard less frequently on the air than Saddam Hussein, Tariq Aziz, Latif Jassim, Dr. Al Anbari or whoever, then this reflected Saudi reluctance to give interviews. (Schleifer's remarks in this volume speak to the same point of coalition forces media, and the reluctance to provide journalists access to stories.) BBC also checked the running orders of all the Arabic Service current affairs programs for any possible distortion of emphasis.

Over time the complaints died away. The thoroughness of the scrutiny and its total failure to confirm the accuracy of the complaints slowly won over all but the most outspoken of the doubters. The determination to carry it out was quite as important as what it revealed. Emotions, too, in the region died down. So why had the complainants been so passionate in their beliefs?

There is no single explanation, and different individuals would give different reasons for objecting. But they are almost certainly a composite of the following ingredients: first, many listeners did not like hearing what they did -- either news that Saddam Hussein was losing, or news that Saddam Hussein was saying anything and was being reported; secondly, some listeners were hearing things that they knew they would never hear on their own media and disliked it on that account or were shocked by what they heard; thirdly, some listeners wanted the BBC to be on their side, whatever side that was, and were disappointed when we were not.; fourthly, some listeners reacted adversely to the nationalities of certain broadcasters on the Arabic Service, assuming that a Palestinian or Jordanian had to be pro-Saddam because of the policies of their respective national leaders; fifthly, some supporters of Saddam Hussein assumed that the BBC was institutionally anti-Saddam because it was reporting news from the allied headquarters, while others assumed that the BBC was pro-Saddam because we reported from Baghdad. Faced with such a tally of conflicting and irreconcilable demands, it was possible only to monitor vigilantly, and take refuge in the solid evidence of the research and even of the correspondence, both of which revealed a solid, majority bedrock of support, approval and trust.

Five Final Lessons

BBC's overall coverage of the Gulf Crisis was not perfect. Of the probable endless list of "things to do" in covering the next war, five lessons seem paramount.

First, there were a lot of aspects that were missed and under-reported -- though seldom in my view the questions about which the complaints are regularly made. Biggest miss was the full realization of the meaning of Bush's doubling of the ground troops in October. Yes, it was covered -- how could it not be? Yet its full implication, that war was inevitable, was given insufficient weight. Did we sufficiently appreciate how the U.S. military had changed its thinking in the aftermath of Vietnam? Or how sophisticated they had become militarily? Secondly, the West treated Saddam Hussein as a political leader working within the recognizable conventions of international politics. He would huff and puff and then withdraw at the last moment because that was what rational leaders would do. The fact that he could emerge strengthened from a late, daring tactical withdrawal made it an obvious Machiavellian maneuver. Thirdly, BBC did not adequately tell listeners/readers what they were NOT being told. It was right to report the official version of events but listeners should have been reminded more often that large areas of activity were being under-reported or not reported at all because there was no information about them. Fourthly, BBC did not tell them the obvious -- you cannot bomb a country and its forces so heavily and for so long without its making a difference. Finally, from time to time BBC took the "Arabists" and the environmentalists too seriously. The scaremongers in both camps said variously that the Arab world would rise up in response to Saddam's call; that terrorism would break out in the fifth column of pro-Saddamism; that the Arab moderates would be overthrown for supporting the Coalition; that the Persian Gulf would be polluted for a generation by the oil pumping by Saddam; etc., etc., etc.

The next war will be covered both more fully and with a greater concern for subtlety, for causal analysis as well as futuristic speculation, for the difference between what we have been told, what we know, what we do not know and what is being deliberately withheld, and with a determination to report the bad news as well as the good.

NOTE: An expanded version of this essay appeared in, John Tusa, *A World in Your Ear*, London: Broadside Books, 1992.

Global Media, The New World Order -- and the Significance of Failure

S. A. Schleifer

The "New World Order" is more than a flight of American presidential rhetoric, though the commanding sound of this phrase disguises the reality to which it alludes.

President Bush first spoke of a "New World Order" in his remarks to a joint session of Congress in September 1990, after Iraq's invasion of Kuwait and the rapid American and allied military buildup in Saudi Arabia. Over the next few months, the President continued to invoke the phrase, and was quoted extensively in all media. With the collapse of the Soviet Union and Eastern Bloc, the phrase came to encompass the post- Cold War world and has been adopted as such even by political forces that have found the phrase suspect.

In strictly political terms of the one superpower in a new multi-polar world guaranteeing that the New World will be spared from future aggressions, the New World Order was born in the Gulf crisis, confirmed in the collapse of the Soviet Union and betrayed in Bosnia. But to think in such strictly political terms is to oversimplify a far more complex and far reaching phenomenon.

For the "New World Order" is the political expression of an emerging global political economy and technological-cultural integration that had been in a state-of-becoming well before August 2, 1990 -- the date of the Iraqi invasion of Kuwait. The rate of that state-of-becoming escalates with each passing development -- and in this context, the Gulf war was a development of momentous significance.

An alternative and seemingly less ominous-sounding description of this emerging phenomenon would be "global culture" or "global civilization," each of which in turn injects into the more obviously political and economic domain a concept having immediate reference to the universal impact of television -- Marshal McLuhan's "Global Village" (A. Smith 1990).

In his time McLuhan was frequently dismissed as an impossible utopian. His vision of an aural-visual universal culture based on electronic broadcast media reintegrating families, neighbors and nations alienated by the individualistic effect of print media was also largely dismissed as unduly optimistic.

A few decades later McLuhan's hopes of television's positive communications effect can indeed easily be challenged as a utopian misreading but the structural component of his vision is increasingly upon us (Alter 1990; Cross-Frontier Broadcasting 1992; V. Smith 1990; Zuckerman 1988). The New World Order can be understood to be emerging as a political dynamic within globally integrative, high- technological information systems. Such systems vary from laser smart bombs, with their extraordinary guidance systems that were seen "going operational" in the Gulf, courtesy of CNN, to CNN itself -- a global news organization with the time, money and capacity to broadcast live from an increasingly large number of places in the world at times of crisis.

These high-tech information systems incorporate any number of computer-satellite linkages that propel global political economy. They affect the movement of men, materials and money as well as provide shallow but increasingly universal perspectives on current events.

Whatever else NWO/Global Culture may be, it is not -- as is too frequently thought by the Arab man-in-the-street -- a euphemism for Western colonialism, white racism or a Christian crusade against Islam. Japan is at the cutting edge of the NWO. It is neither Western, white nor Christian; its troops did not participate in the coalition only because the Japanese constitution forbids such participation. But the Japanese were major bankrollers of the coalition. And vast amounts of Arab, Indian Muslim, Malay and Bruneian wealth fuels the economy of the global culture and finances much of its most dynamic sectors. Japanese, Arab and Muslim investors are all intrinsic elements of the emerging New World Order. Japanese technology (followed by Taiwan) is a major component of high-tech information systems and the Japanese have acquired major stakes in the entertainment side of global media, just as Arab capital with the recent purchase of UPI and the establishment of a satellite-driven, Arabic-language global television station has moved into the journalistic side of global media.

Nevertheless, there is a Western point of origin for almost all the fads, fashions and global perspectives that bounce about electronically and are absorbed elsewhere to the degree they don't obviously and outrageously violate local traditional standards. Modern secular Western culture is at the heart of the New World Order.

Even some of the most visibly agitated opponents of the globalization of modern secular Western culture have themselves been shaped by it, and the style of their opposition to modern Western culture reflects its influence.

Consider the Iranian fundamentalist youth enrolled in the Leninist-sounding Revolutionary Guards, waving clenched fists, wearing U.S.-style field jackets and sporting five-day-growth beards. All of the symbols and images they employed were acquired, largely courtesy of pre-revolutionary Iranian TV, from the global culture's parade of the symbols, gestures and paraphernalia of American New Left protest, the civil rights movement and Latin American guerrilla radical chic. They did not derive from the Islamic heritage.

The NWO is an evolving system of global political economy and technological-cultural integration based on high-tech information systems that are continuously evolving toward more and more effective, complex and rapid integration. We are dealing with an emerging universal order where boundaries are demarcated not by the presence of garrisons but by the presence and extent of satellites and ground station activity. Being an actor in the NWO does not require the ability to man a military outpost on somebody else's territory, or rather on territory that is still somebody else's for the time being, *so much as it is requires having means to participate in the total information system effectively*.

The failure of Saddam Hussein to understand this led in part to his profound miscalculation of the Global Culture's probable response to his occupation of Kuwait. As Boylan earlier in this work illustrated, Egyptian cartoonists were quick to exploit the miscalculation.

A similar lack of comprehension afflicted the Joint Forces, the name given to Saudi and other Arab and Islamic military contingents serving as part of the coalition in Saudi Arabia. The failure of the political establishment of those Arab states participating in the anti-Iraqi coalition to understand the information system led to an Arab Joint Forces media policy that resulted in political disaster, despite the overwhelming military victory of the coalition.

The American political establishment could not avert the disaster because it did not recognize the critical consequences of the failure of the Joint Forces' media policy. Since our critical understanding (like our vocabulary in cultural lag theory) can often trail behind the technologically mediated political culture that we inhabit, American and British media critics tended to miss all of this.

They focused their analyses upon purely domestic issues -- rather than those of global implication -- such as the effect of media coverage upon American popular support for Desert Shield and Desert Storm, and the relationship between that coverage and the tight management of news coverage by the U.S. military. At best, they focused on the dependence of world media upon CNN for coverage of the conflict.

Media criticism varied from the predictable anti-Americanism and naive analysis typified by the special Gulf war issue in *Media Development*, 1991, to the more sophisticated treatment of similar ground by the contributors to *The Media at War: The Press and the Persian Gulf Conflict*, to the introspective and professionally astute observations by Ed Fouhy.

In many ways Saddam Hussein miscalculated in much the same manner (but with none of the good intentions) as those British Muslim protesters who burned copies of Salman Rushdie's book before British TV cameras after months of trying to make the British Establishment understand why Rushdie's *Satanic Verses* was so offensive to Muslim sensibility (Webster 1990).

When British Muslim immigrants from the Indian subcontinent burn a book, anyone who grew up in the crucible of modern Western culture may immediately recall the newsreel image of Nazi bookburnings, however unfair the comparison may be.

Webster argues that the Nazi bookburnings by an all-powerful, totalitarian state were in stark contrast to the British bookburning by a powerless and ignored racial and religious minority. The real issue, confused by media coverage of the Muslim bookburning, was what is ultimately, truly sacred and what is not.

Religion is no longer seen by most Westerners to be particularly relevant to modern life. But the instinct for the sacred remains so intrinsic that modern

Western consciousness and particularly the consciousness of journalists -- members of the scribal class par excellence -- will invest literature, and in particular the modern novel (the work, for instance, of a Salman Rushdie or in Egypt of an Alaa Hamed), with a sacred quality.

A formerly unknown Egyptian novelist, Hamed was sentenced to eight years' imprisonment on December 25, 1991, by Egyptian Security (Martial Law) Court for threatening national unity and social peace and for "mocking divine religions," which would be an Arabic political equivalent of blasphemy, and which Egyptian law considers a criminal offense. Early in May 1992 a different court acquitted Hamed of a similar charge. The original sentencing must be confirmed by Egypt's prime minister before it can be implemented (Napoli 1992). In the cases of both Rushdie and Hamed, it was the "bookburning" and not the sacrilegious book, that was perceived more immediately within NWO global culture as "sacrilegious."

Nazi bonfires. That's the image conjured for most senior editors, publishers, and TV news producers, most of whom are over 40. The same image emerges for this author, despite the profound offense he took at Rushdie's conscious act of blasphemy.

But the pious Pakistani immigrant in England does not share that image, because the Nazi experience as an "idea," or fact that is absorbed into the historic assumptions of the modern West, means nearly nothing to him. He is part of the NWO by virtue of his interaction with global media, but he does not know the rules.

In the global culture news editors everywhere are locked into international news services and share to an amazing degree the same idea of what is newsworthy (Serbeny 1984).

In contrast to Arab and Islamic culture at the periphery of global civilization, there are the Japanese, profoundly conscious of themselves, of their history, their culture and, almost to a point of embarrassment, their homogeneity. But every Japanese high school boy masters Western history, and with far more intensity than the subject is approached by most American college students. One cannot imagine any contemporary educated Japanese journalist or politician having trouble appreciating the sort of appalling associations that attach in Western consciousness to Hitler or Hitlerian behavior.

But Saddam Hussein had no perception of this. On Aug. 2 when the Iraqi Army rolled across the border into Kuwait it did so with barely any but the most transparent of efforts to mask this land grab. Its unveiled ruthlessness immediately reminded any middle-aged or older person (and not just George Bush) whose consciousness has been shaped by global culture of Hitler's armies pouring into Poland or Holland.

But even the masters of high-tech information systems do not understand the implications of an emerging global culture and, in particular, of the dangers of uneven participation in that culture.

From mid-August to mid-September 1990, this author worked in Saudi Arabia as an NBC News field producer covering the build-up of Desert Shield. He was struck at the time by an extraordinary lack of equilibrium in access and coverage.

Every day the U.S. armed forces Public Affairs office provided the international press covering the build-up with a minimum of eight story opportunities with American troops. In that same period the Joint Forces -- the Arab-Islamic contingent in the coalition, including Saudi, Egyptian, Syrian, Kuwaiti, Moroccan, Senegalese and Pakistani troops -- provided a total of eight stories for the entire month. That's eight stories per day about the American buildup and only eight stories a month about the 100,000 Arab-Islamic forces holding down the front-line, far in advance of American forces at that time.

Since the British forces provided an average of two story opportunities a day, this established an Anglo-American total of approximately 10 a day to the Joint Forces' eight stories a month. According to colleagues who stayed on for the duration, this ratio continued and even worsened.

The implications of this imbalance must be considered within two contexts. First, neither CNN nor any other international news organizations were in Kuwait when the Iraqis struck. And the Iraqis -- however hospitable they were to CNN and other global journalists in Baghdad -- never allowed access to Kuwait either during the first days of invasion, when looting and rape were followed by the rounding up of foreign hostages, or later on during the conflict, when Kuwaiti nationals suspected of resistance activities were tortured, executed or deported to Iraq.

While there were a few print stories about the invasion that contained eye-witness accounts taken from refugees or by telephone calls from Kuwait, there were no vivid on-the-scene accounts, no vivid pictures, no round-the-clock electronic images, nor any flood of newspaper stories. There were only some hazy, quickly shot home videos of a few burning cars and buildings -- fuzzy images of Kuwait City that faded away after a few days.

At the same time, round-the-clock coverage of the American military build-up in Saudi Arabia was transmitted throughout the world. Arab and Islamic television stations rarely if ever cover foreign news with their own crews and rely instead on international TV agencies or CNN for foreign news pictures. Even if Egyptian, other Arab states and Islamic TV stations had sent news teams to Saudi Arabia, they would have faced the same problem as Western media: the severely limited access to the Arab-Islamic Joint Forces under Saudi command.

Since there were hardly any TV reports of Arab and Islamic forces building up and digging in as part of the allied coalition, the vivid images were of neither the Iraqi aggression nor of the pro-Kuwaiti Arab and Islamic response. They were of a seemingly exclusive American and European buildup, seen day after day -- out of context of the Iraqi aggression and of the Arab-Islamic response to that aggression. These continuous images were also projected to the Muslim world -- in some cases, fewer than 30 years away from their own bitter memories of European military occupation (Algeria) or the 40-year collective memory of the West's imposition of a European Jewish settler state in Palestine. These were the elements in Arab and Islamic collective memory that "read" the out-of-context and therefore misleading images of Gulf crisis coverage into the occupation of Arabia -- the Prophet's homeland -- by the forces of Western colonialism.

These misleading, out-of-context images flashing continuously across the global consciousness (through little fault of the media itself) made Saddam Hussein's case for him. For the duration of the crisis, Radio Baghdad broadcast a stream of accusations: That American troops were in the sacred city of Mekkah directing security around The Haram, the Holy Mosque that contains the Kaaba; that American women soldiers were practicing prostitution in Mekkah, as well as in other parts of Saudi Arabia; and that American troops were also deployed in Medina.

Given the focus on what increasingly appeared -- courtesy of out-of-context global TV -- to be an Anglo-American military occupation of Saudi Arabia, Baghdad Radio acquired credibility. This was all the easier for Radio Baghdad since no consistent or significant attempt to rebut these charges on a global basis was made by Saudi Arabia until the outbreak of fighting in mid-January 1991. That was when the author returned to the Kingdom to direct the World Muslim News Service, an emergency multi-media unit for the Muslim World League, an international semi-official Saudi body based in Mekkah (Davidian 1991; Shadroui 1991).

Davidian, in one of the few press reports on the activities of WMNS, noted that while Westerners may not understand the outrage of Muslims hearing (and believing) the Radio Baghdad accusations, neither had the media (pro-coalition Arab and Islamic media as well as global media) countered the reports. This left the Muslims around the world with only the incorrect version of the story.

WMNS was established by the Muslim World League in response to the increasingly serious waves of massive pro-Iraqi demonstrations in countries like Morocco and Pakistan where the political establishment was strongly pro-Saudi, but were forced by the intensity of the demonstrations to minimize any bold role for their armed forces in Saudi Arabia in the last days leading up to Desert Storm.

WMNS's news product -- finished TV field reports or "spots" in Arabic and English -- were transmitted via ARABSAT to all Arab countries and were rebroadcast in Egypt, the Gulf states and Morocco. Video copies of the WMNS reports were also distributed to CNN, Visnews and the American, British and European TV news pools. The sound portion of the video reports was copied on audio tape for rebroadcast by Radio Free Kuwait operating out of Saudi Arabia, and for a joint American-Saudi Armed Forces Radio Service broadcasting to Iraqi troops in and near Kuwait.

But WMNS was a shoe-string operation; its product, however earnest and sophisticated, was but a drop in the media bucket, and it had begun five months too late.

In a background report submitted to the Muslim World League, this author, in his capacity as WMNS executive producer, defined the problem:

> The purpose of the World Muslim News Service (WMNS) is to generate daily coverage of the Islamic dimension of the Gulf war with TV field reports, still photography for daily newspapers and other publications, and news feature stories for wire copy news services.
>
> This is of critical importance since the overall impression in the Muslim world derived from global media coverage of the war as well as from the extensive propaganda work undertaken by the Iraqi regime is mostly negative to Saudi Arabia and demoralizing to those Arab and Islamic countries allied to Saudi Arabia in the Coalition.
>
> Despite the fact that ulama from all over the Muslim World support Saudi Arabia; despite the fact that troops from more than half a dozen Arab and Islamic countries are serving on Saudi soil; despite the fact that the Saudi and Kuwaiti air forces have participated fully with the other Allied Forces in the first phase of the battle for the liberation of Kuwait that is now underway; the Muslim peoples throughout the Islamic world or in residence in large numbers in Europe and the Americans are unaware of the Islamic dimension to this struggle, if not hostile to Saudi Arabia and the cause of Kuwaiti liberation.
>
> On the other hand, the most despicable lies about the status of the Holy Places here in Hijaz are circulated by Baghdad media throughout the Muslim world without rebuttal, as well as the Iraqi claim that this is an American war against the Arabs and the Muslims. The fact that this is a *Jihad* by Arab and Islamic forces, first to defend Saudi Arabia from aggression and then to liberate Kuwait, has been eclipsed by the absence of almost any Arab and Islamic element in the coverage transmitted by global news organizations to the Islamic world (Schleifer 1991).

What was to be finally set up by the Saudis with very limited resources and too late into the crisis had been proposed to the highest echelon of the United States

Information Service in Washington by the author via American embassy channels in Cairo in mid-September. Washington was not interested. Its response was that an Islamic-oriented field news unit was the proper concern of the Muslim partners in the coalition, not of the United States. But that was to ask the problem to come up with the solution.

From the Kuwaiti perspective the Gulf war began on August 2, 1990, with the Iraqi invasion. What happened in mid-January 1991 -- Desert Storm -- was the counter-offensive launched by the powerful friends and allies of Kuwait and included participation by Kuwaiti air force and infantry. But because of the circumstances of global news coverage and the varying abilities of the coalition forces to make effective use of that coverage, even the West's own perception of when the Gulf war began -- with Desert Storm, on Jan. 17th -- yields unconsciously to the Iraqi definition of who initiated the conflict.

It would be as if history had recorded Dec. 7, 1941, the day Japan bombed Pearl Harbor, as the beginning of World War II -- and not the German invasion of Poland in 1939.

The stunning military victory by the American-led coalition appears to have minimized the damage. But the inability or unwillingness of the Arab forces allied in that coalition, and the failure of Washington to take corrective measures in light of that unwillingness or inability to respond to the requirements of global coverage, gave most of the Muslim world's streets to Saddam Hussein.

The reverberations of that extraordinary political failure may yet return to haunt the Arab and Islamic world.

Appendix A

SpaceNet Service

As with ARABSAT, SpaceNet consists of a space segment and a ground segment. The space segment includes:

1. One direct TV broadcast transponder or DVTB transponder. The receiver operates on the 6GHz or C-band. The transmitter operates on 2.5GHz or S-band Therefore, the DTVB transponder operates on C-S-band. It has a capacity of one community TV channel medium power which provides a minimum of 41 dbw over the Arab Region (ITU Handbook, Geneva, 1988, p. 585). The SpaceNet channel is available from ARABSAT satellite 1-A and operates in geosynchronous orbit at longitude 19 degrees east. The DVTB transponder is identified as number 26 since the spacecraft has 25 other transponders of low power for telephone services and the exchange of TV programs. These 25 transponders operate on the C-C band.
2. Two Tracking, Telemetry, Telecommand, and Monitoring (TTCM) stations. The primary TTCM station is near Riyadh, Saudi Arabia, and the secondary TTCM station is near Tunis, Tunisia.

The ground segment consists of the following:

1. An earth station transmitter owned and installed by the Arab Republic's Egyptian National Telecommunications Organization (ARENTO) in the center for satellite earth stations (teleport) at Maadi, Cairo, Egypt.
2. A microwave link installed and maintained by ARENTO sends SpaceNet programs originating at the Maspero TV building to the earth station transmitter (uplink) at Maadi.
3. 2.5GHz band S-band TVRO, three meter reception dishes throughout Arab, African, and European countries are distributed as follows:

TVROs installed by ERTU in Arab countries:

- In the TV building of Kuwait (Kuwait City), Abu Dhabi (Ahu Dhabi), Oman (Muscat), Qatar (Doha City), Yemen (Aden), Sanaa (Yemen) and Libya (Tripoli).
- The two palaces of King Fahd in Riyadh, Saudi Arabia.
- The palace of Sheikh Zayed, President of the United Arab Emirates, in Abu Dhabi.

- The residence of Ali Abdullah Saleh, President of Yemen.

- The residence of Sultan Qaboos in Muscat, Oman.

TVROs installed by ERTU in Africa:

- The TV building of Kenya (Nairobi), Djibouti, Chad, Zambia (Lusaka), Congo (Brazzaville), Niger (Niami), Uganda (Kampala), Zaire (Kinshasa), and Guinea (Konkary).

TVROs installed by ERTU in Europe:

- The residence of the Egyptian ambassador in Paris.
- The residence of the Egyptian ambassador in London.
- The end terminal of the TV cable company Videotron in London.

In addition to the TVROs mentioned above, approximately two thousand TVROs have been installed in Saudi Arabia by individuals (ERTU report) and many others installed by individuals in Europe.

TVROs installed by ERTU in Egypt:

- The TV center in Aswan to be used as a standby for the Cairo-Aswan microwave link.
- The TV center in Farafrah Oasis to be used as a standby for Cairo
- Bahaira - Farafrah microwave links.
- The TV center in Saint Catherine to transmit the SpaceNet programs to the local population. No ERTU microwave link is available.
- In Habata in order to transmit to military forces in the Western Sahara. No ERTU microwave link is available.
- The earth station transmitter in Maadi, the microwave link for SpaceNet programs originating in Maspero to the earth station transmitter at Maadi, and the above TVROs for the ground segment of SpaceNet.

Appendix B

SpaceNet Programming

News: Twelve percent of the total weekly programming. Included are international and national news presentations and news analysis.

Children's Programs: Children's programs account for fourteen percent of the total weekly programming. Popular programs include Cinema El-Atfal, Boogy wa Tumtum, and Atfal Al-Omda Al-Ali. Other programs show children different countries of the world, Egyptian tourist sites, and the arts.

Cultural Programs: Cultural programs account for twenty-four percent of the weekly programming. Shows include:

- Technologia -- a 30-minute scientific program designed to simplify complicated scientific information for the audience.
- Health program -- a 20-30-minute documentary style program that features professors of the Faculty of Medicine to review the latest medical and health news.
- Women's program -- These are generally 30-minute programs about problems of working women as well as homemakers.
- Dunya El Saheya -- a 30-minute program featuring tourism in Egypt through a format of meetings and documentary films about tourism. The program invites foreigners and Egyptians to visit the ancient Egyptian monuments.
- Al Musica Al Arabia -- a 55-minute presentation of Arabic music with a musical and historical analysis.
- Omsya Thaqafiya -- a 30-minute presentation of issues and problems of literature. The program is designed to enrich the intellectual and literary movement.
- Opera 91 -- performance of operas and classical music.
- Mosafer Zadoho Al Khayal -- a 30-minute tourism documentary-style program to show natural and ancient wonders of Egypt. It also presents meetings with Egyptian people, tourists, and officials in the field.
- Eiadet Al-Qanah Al-Talta -- a weekly 15-minute program of medical information for patients featuring selected medical cases to be treated.
- Mazika -- a weekly 30-minute program dealing with special subjects, particularly musical instruments and offers instruction in their use as well as explanation of the technology of modern music recording.
- Yoekad Fi -- a 15-minute program featuring scenes of social, literary, and cultural events.
- Maa Martabet Al Sharaf -- this unusual 15-minute program records

the master and Ph.D. dissertation discussions in the universities.

- Cinema' eyat -- a 30-minute program dealing with artistic and theatrical events and international and Egyptian festivals.

- Dakkat Al Masrah -- a program that deals with the theatrical and artistic events and international and Egyptian festivals.

- Ta'asim Salam -- a 30-minute biographical program to acquaint viewers with events and important personalities who have been honored.

- Qemam Marayyah -- a 30-minute program featuring scholars of literature, thought, and culture who have received honorary certificates.

- Al-Rasm Bil Kalimat -- a 15-minute interview program featuring cultural, literary, and artistic personalities in Egypt.

Religious Programs: These programs account for about three percent of the weekly programming and feature religious leaders who explain the Quran and Sunah. They include: Nadith El Koah (5 mins.), Nadwah Lel Ra'ai (40 mins.), Leq'a al Gomma (featuring Sheikh Al Sharawi, a very popular religious leader) (30 mins.), and Al Egaz el Elmy fi Al Quran (15 mins.).

Sports Programs: These programs account for five to fifteen percent of the total weekly programming.

Entertainment Programs: These programs account for about 42 percent of the total weekly broadcast materials:

- Amani wa Aghani -- a 60-minute program dealing with youth problems.

- Hakawy al Qahawi -- a 40-minute program presenting the Egyptian artistic heritage through meetings with people in cafes.

- Taxi Al Sahra -- new Arabic films, plays, and foreign films along with meetings with the actors in these works.

- Sherit Al Zekrayat -- distinguished figures in art, literature and science.

- Fi Beitona Negm -- a 30-minute program featuring a famous star at home in a dialogue about his/her life and the important issues in the field.

- Mehna wa Le'ba - a 30-minute program featuring a sports figure and an ordinary citizen working in a similar job. It presents a dialogue between a citizen and the professional about changing places

- Negum wa Laken -- a 30-minute program about stars and their work.

- Ostazy al Aziz Shokran -- a 30-minute program featuring public characters deserving thanks.
- Bein Al Mehna wa al Hawayah -- an entertaining 30-minute program showing examples of writers and artists, their hobbies, and their jobs.
- Qabl al Montage -- a 10 minute program including comic snaps or outtakes (i.e., "bloopers").
- Adam Bedun Hawa'a -- This program interviews single people and questions them about their future marital plans and how they cope without a partner.
- Tom fi Hayati -- a 30-minute program that presents a full day in the life of a famous character, examines how he/she spends time, and solicits his/her opinions.
- Al-Menagemati -- This program features a famous actor and reviews predictions with him/her in a comic way.
- Da-awah Lel Hob -- This program features discussions about the important issues in love and conducts dialogues about love with important journalists and authors.

Appendix C

SpaceNet International

Service to Egyptian facilities outside Egypt:

- Egyptian embassies and consulates in Arab, African, and European countries as well as several Asian countries such as Pakistan and India.
- Cultural offices belonging to the Egyptian Ministry of Education.
- Press offices.
- Egyptian and Arab clubs.
- Egyptian companies, e.g., export/import firms and airline offices.
- Cable TV companies in Europe.
- African TV organizations for retransmission via their national VHF and UHF transmitters (gratis).
- Arab TV organizations.

Domestic service:

- Populated areas outside the reach of the existing national microwave network, such as Saint Catherine in South Sinai, three kilometers above sea level.
- Populated areas where television reception is weak, such as Al Mathani, Al Zeitoon, Neguila, Alam Al Rum, Al Shebeika, and Ras Al Hekma -- all are along the northwestern coast. Areas near the Red Sea receiving SpaceNet include Hamata, Abugusson, Bir Shalatein, and Halaib Marsa Alam. Sir Gifgafa, Al Qusseima, Nakhi, Kuntella, Abu Zeneima, Wadi Sidr, and Ras Al Nakab - all in Sinai -- also receive SpaceNet.
- New Communities, such as Al Asher Men Ramadan, New Salehia, New Naboria, Wadi al Natrun, and Al Sadat City.
- New tourist regions, such as the tourist villages near the Red Sea and the Mediterranean Sea.
- Egyptian military forces residing in remote areas, petroleum companies in the desert, isolated mining areas, and industrial concentrations in desert areas.

SpaceNet also assisted in the preparations for the second stage of individual reception of direct TV broadcast, expected for the second generation of ARABSAT. SpaceNet is also providing television broadcast engineers with the experience of broadcast by satellites and provides for back-up of existing microwave links.

Appendix D

Al-Ahram, Al-Akhbar and Al-Wafd

Frequency of Topics

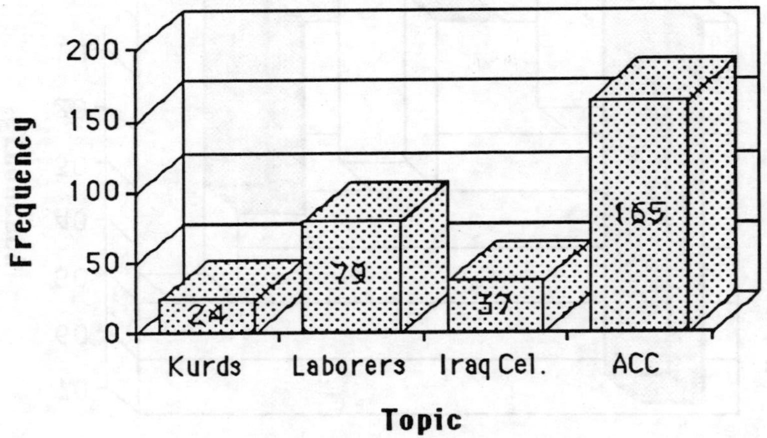

Coverage by Year *Al-Ahram*
Kurds

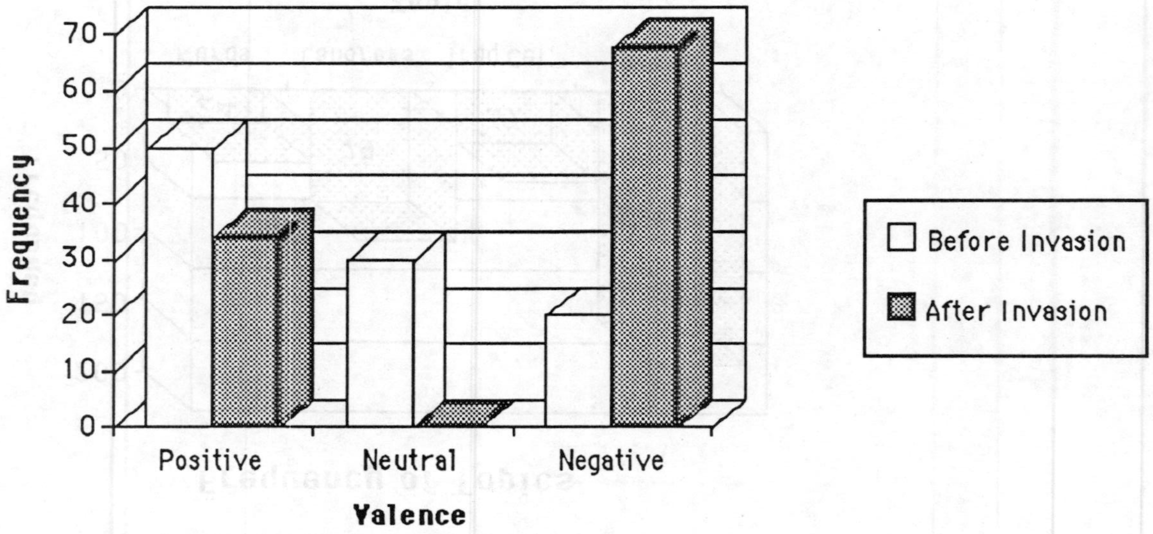

Coverage by Year *Al-Akhbar*
Kurds

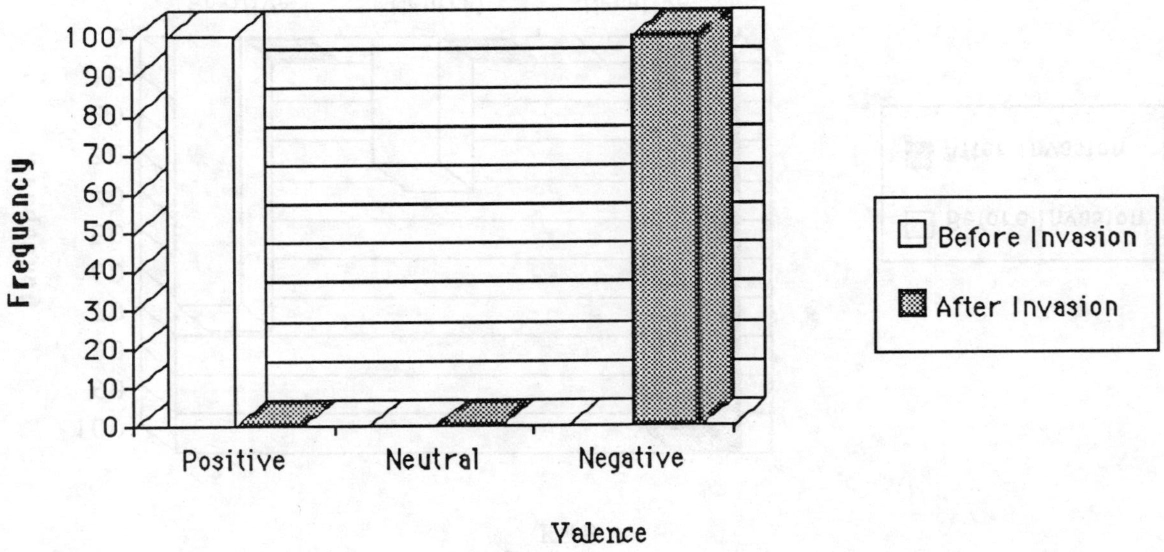

Coverage by Year Al-T·SW
Kurds

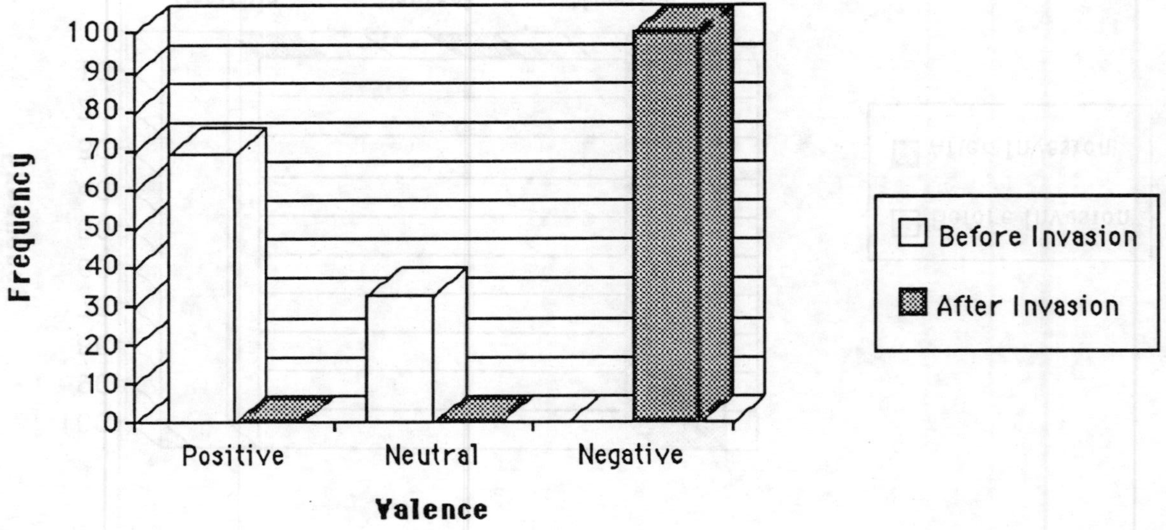

Coverage by Year : *Al-Ahram*
Laborers' Crisis in Iraq

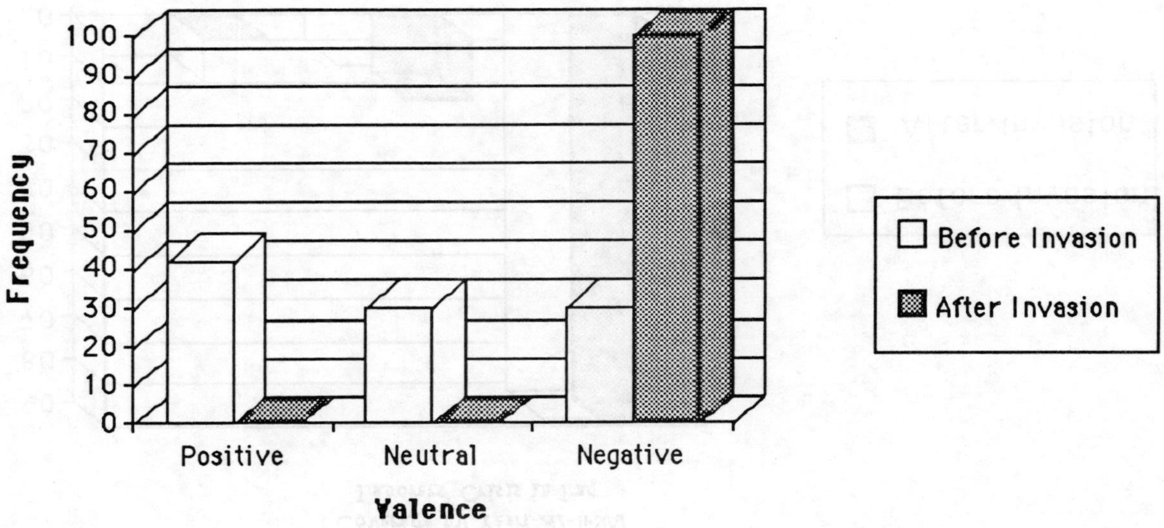

Coverage by Year Al-IT·SW
Laborers' Crisis in Iraq

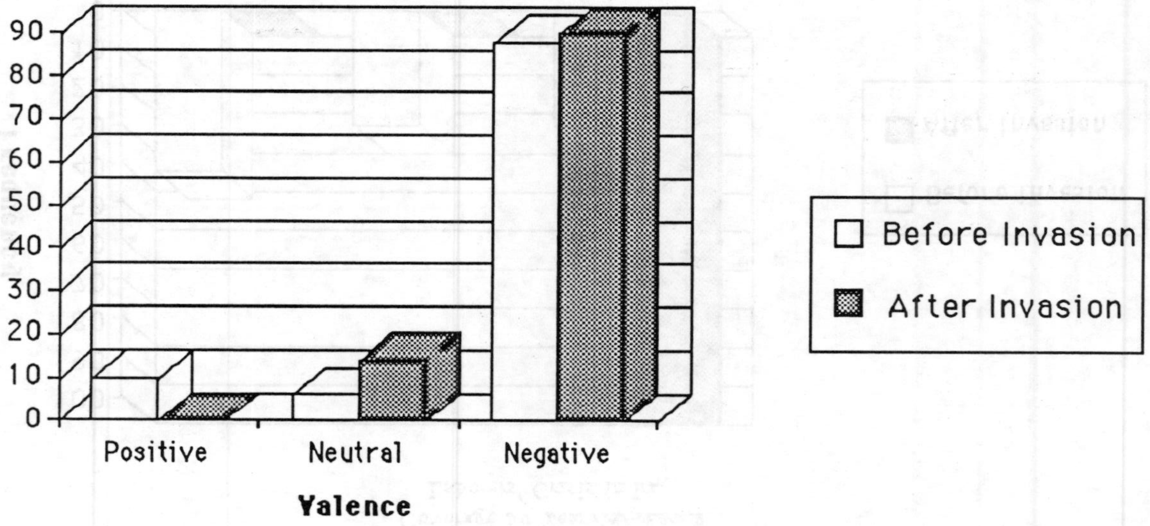

Coverage by Year *Al-Ahram*
Arab Cooperation Council

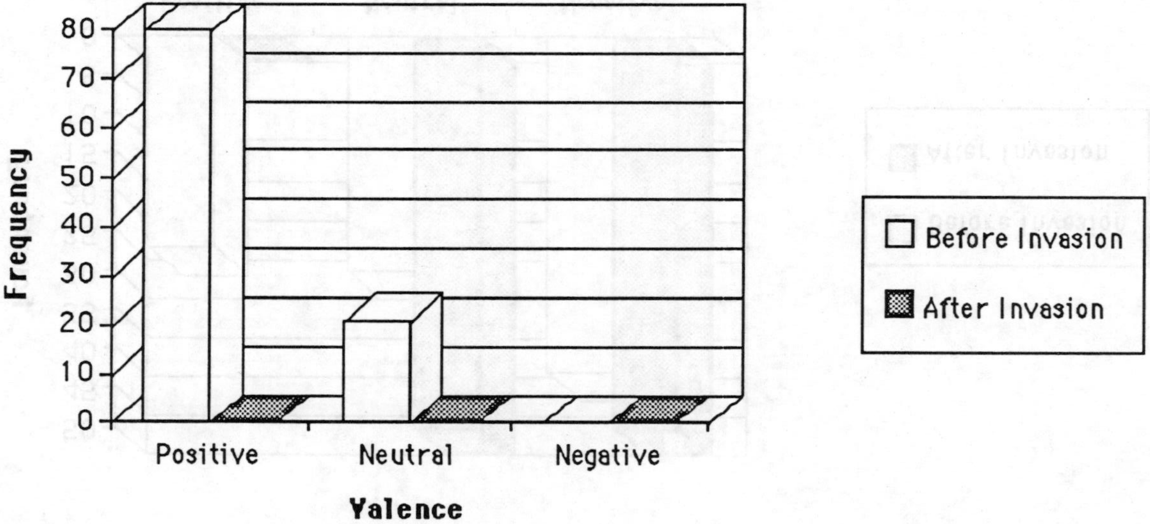

Coverage by Year *Al-Akhbar*
Laborers' Crisis in Iraq

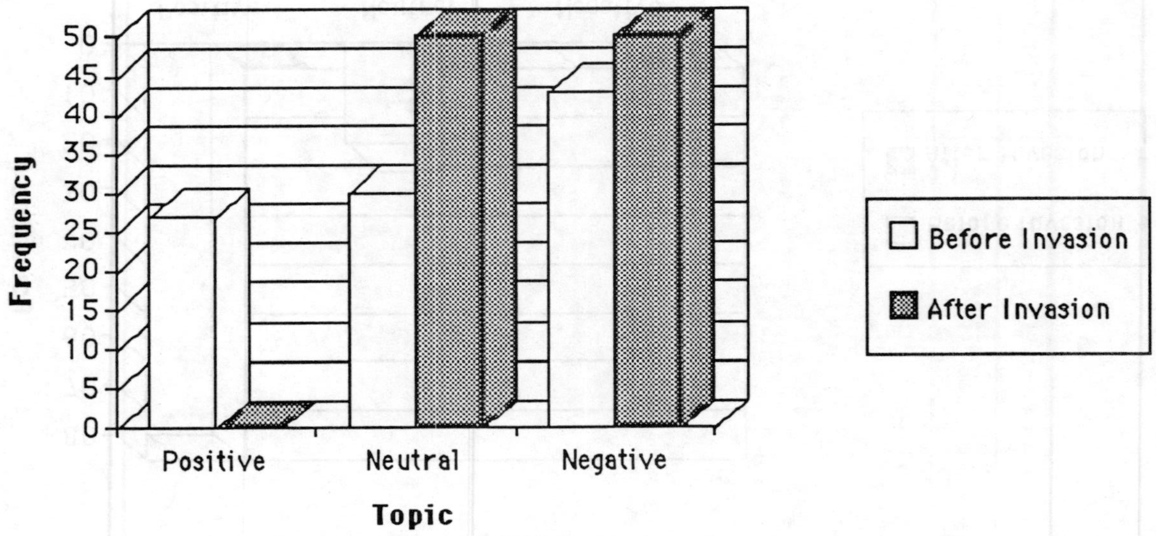

Coverage by Year: *Al-Akhbar*
Arab Cooperation Council

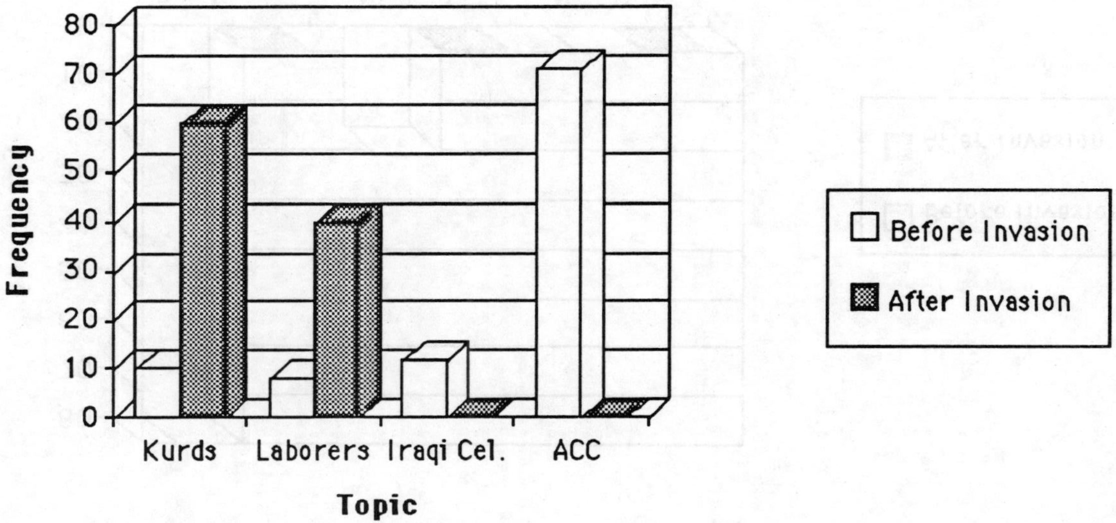

Coverage by Year Al-[illegible]
Arab Cooperation Council

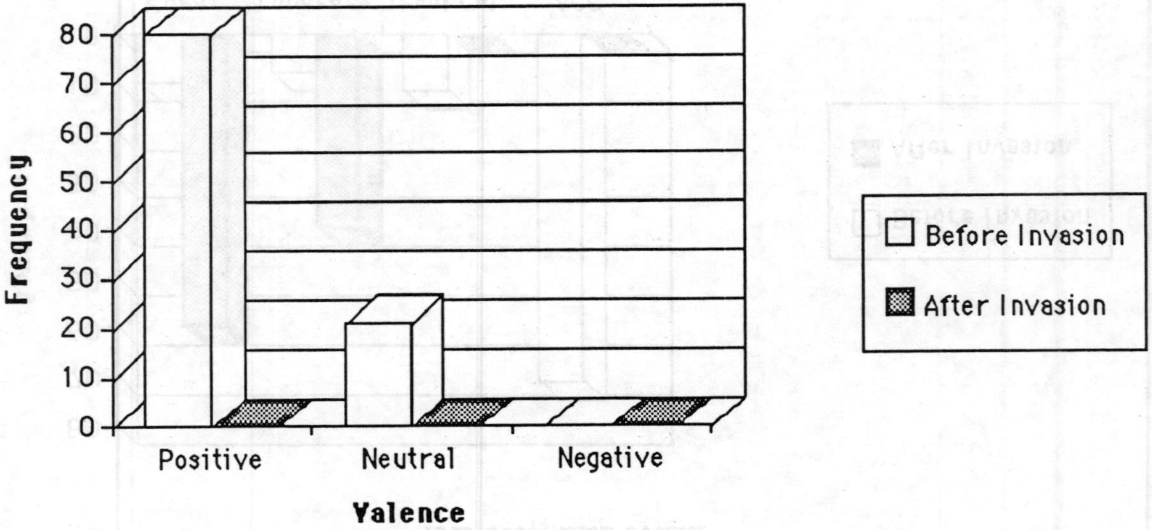

Frequency of Topics by Year

Al-Ahram

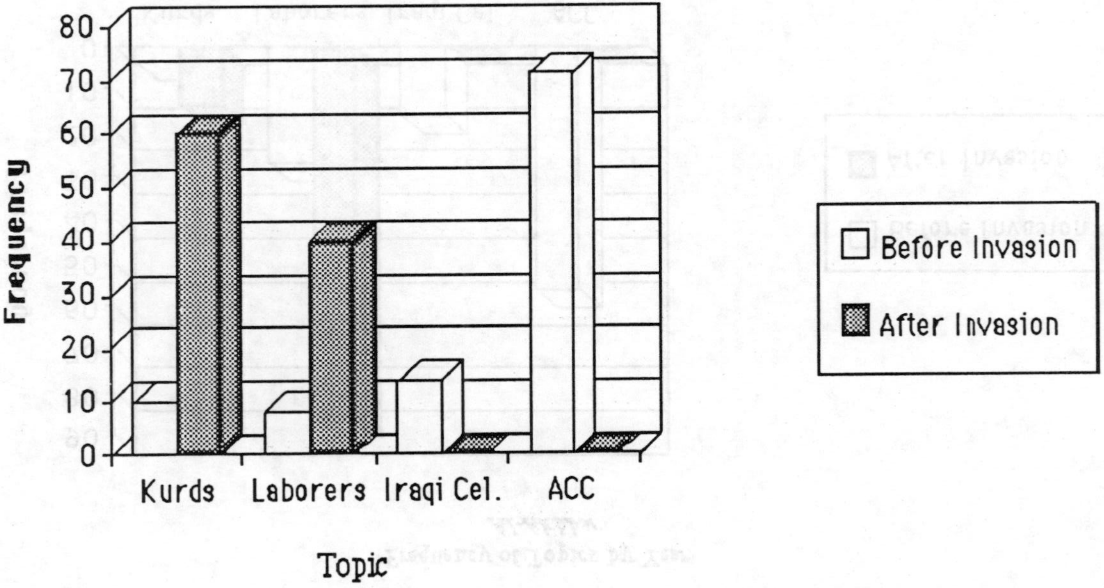

Frequency of Topics by Year
Al-Akhbar

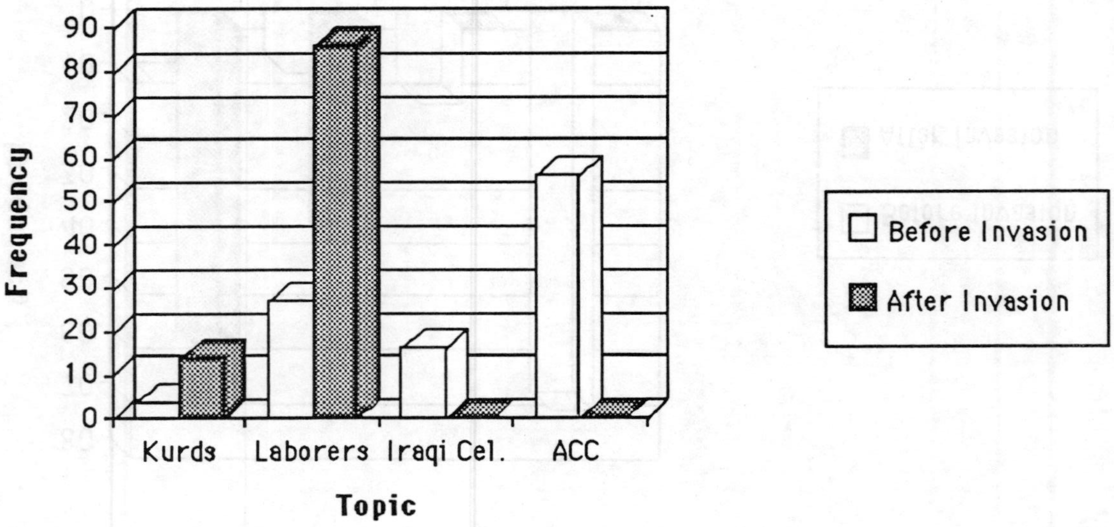

Frequency of topics by Year

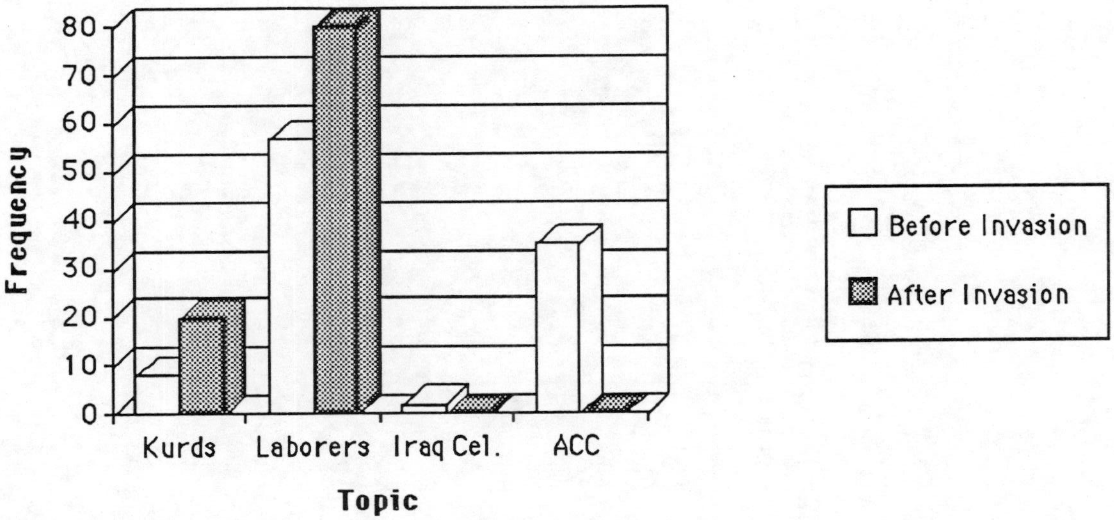

Appendix E

Front Page *Al-Ahram* Coverage

Date	Total no. of stories on the front page	No. of stories on the Gulf Crisis (FP)	%
Jan. 14	15	13	87
Jan. 15	15	14	93.5
Jan. 16	9	8	89
Jan. 17	7	7	100
Jan. 18	9	9	100
Jan. 19	9	9	100
Jan. 20	12	12	100
Jan. 21	14	10	71.5
Jan. 22	10	9	90
Jan. 23	14	11	78
Jan. 24	12	10	84
Jan. 25	10	10	100
Jan. 26	13	12	92.5
Jan. 27	12	11	92
Jan. 28	15	11	73.5
Jan. 29	9	5	55.5
Jan. 30	14	9	64.5
Jan. 31	7	7	100
Feb. 1	12	10	83.5
Feb. 2	10	9	90
Feb. 3	13	7	54
Feb. 4	12	7	58.5
Feb. 5	14	8	57.5
Feb. 6	11	6	54.5
Feb. 7	13	10	77
Feb. 8	11	8	73
Feb. 9	14	11	78.5
Feb. 10	14	8	57.5
Feb. 11	13	11	85
Feb. 12	9	5	55.5
Feb. 13	13	12	92.5
Feb. 14	13	11	85
Feb. 15	11	8	73
Feb. 16	9	8	89
Feb. 17	10	8	80
Feb. 18	12	8	67
Feb. 19	16	6	37.5
Feb. 20	12	7	58.5
Feb. 21	14	8	57
Feb. 22	11	11	100
Feb. 23	12	8	67
Feb. 24	14	10	71.5
Feb. 25	11	9	82
Feb. 26	8	7	87
Feb. 27	13	10	77
Feb. 28	13	9	69.5

Front Page *Al-Wafd* Coverage

Date	Total no. of stories on the front page	No. of stories on the Gulf Crisis (FP)	%
Jan. 14	25	12	48
Jan. 15	27	21	78
Jan. 16	20	14	70
Jan. 17	15	12	80
Jan. 18	18	16	89
Jan. 19	16	15	94
Jan. 20	14	12	86
Jan. 21	18	13	72.5
Jan. 22	29	17	59
Jan. 23	23	18	78.5
Jan. 24	18	13	72.5
Jan. 25	23	19	83
Jan. 26	23	22	96
Jan. 27	17	17	100
Jan. 28	22	15	69
Jan. 29	30	23	77
Jan. 30	22	14	64
Jan. 31	19	16	84
Feb. 1	22	14	64
Feb. 2	27	24	89
Feb. 3	24	14	58
Feb. 4	18	14	78
Feb. 5	21	9	43
Feb. 6	25	17	68
Feb. 7	18	12	67
Feb. 8	24	17	71
Feb. 9	21	13	62
Feb. 10	21	12	57
Feb. 11	25	17	68
Feb. 12	25	15	60
Feb. 13	21	15	71.5
Feb. 14	15	11	73.5
Feb. 15	26	17	65.5
Feb. 16	20	14	70
Feb. 17	20	13	65
Feb. 18	25	14	56
Feb. 19	25	12	48
Feb. 20	18	11	61
Feb. 21	17	11	65
Feb. 22	21	17	81
Feb. 23	19	18	95
Feb. 24	23	17	74
Feb. 25	18	18	100
Feb. 26	15	12	80
Feb. 27	16	13	81.5
Feb. 28	18	15	84

Front Page *Al-Shaab* Coverage

Date	Total no. of stories on the front page	No. of stories on the Gulf Crisis (FP)	%
Jan. 15	4	4	100
Jan. 22	5	4	80
Jan. 29	12	9	75
Feb. 5	13	10	77
Feb. 12	12	8	66.5
Feb. 19	20	13	65
Feb. 26	12	11	91.5

Direction of the News

Direction	*Al-Ahram*		*Al-Wafd*		*Al-Shaab*	
	Freq.	%	Freq.	%	Freq.	%
Pro-Saddam	5	1.66	15	3.04	14	23.72
Anti-Saddam	295	98.33	478	96.95	45	76.27
Total No. of Articles	300	100	493	100	59	100

Fig. 23

Subject Matter of the Story

Subject Matter of the Story

Subject Category	*Al-Ahram*		*AL Wafd*		*Al-Shaab*	
	Freq.	%	Freq.	%	Freq.	%
1. Humanitarian	2	44	30	4.5	1	1.9
2. Anti-US	1	.22	3	.45	10	19.2
3. Statements Supporting Saddam	-	-	15	2.2	8	15.3
4. Report of Military Affairs	21	4.7	74	11.2	9	17.3
5. Arab United Position	14	3.1	10	1.5	1	1.9
6. Mubarak's statements	28	6.2	14	2.1	-	-
7. Editorial	20	4.4	32	4.8	2	3.83
8. Pro-US	15	2.8	3	.45	-	-
9. Official US statments	22	4.9	29	4.4	-	-
10. Report of Military	112	25.1	152	23.1	1	1.9

Subject Matter of the Story

Subject Category	*Al-Ahram*		*AL Wafd*		*Al-Shaab*	
	Freq.	%	Freq.	%	Freq.	%
11. Pro-peace	42	9.4	41	6.2	-	-
12. Anti-peace	5	1.1	13	1.9	-	-
13. War Costs, Loses for All Sides	10	2.2	74	11.2	2	3.83
14. Re-building Kuwait	4	.89	9	1.3	-	-
15. Terrorist Actions against Allied Forces and Israel	1	.22	18	2.7	9	17.3
16. Iraqi People's Reaction	15	3.3	26	3.9	4	7.6
17. Saddam's statements	9	2	14	2.1	1	1.9
18. Progress of Peace Negotiations	66	14.7	62	9.4	-	-
19. Bush's statements	44	9.8	50	7.6	4	7.6
20 Other	18	4.03	14	2.1	-	-

REFERENCES

References

-- "A Summary of the Radio and TV Union's achievements in 1990/1991." The Radio and TV Union, Office of the President of the Trustees Council, 3-5.

-- Abdulla, Rasha A. (1992). "The Effects of CNN on Egyptian News," unpublished research report, the American University in Cairo, Dept. of Journalism and Mass Communication.

-- Abu-Argoub, I. A. (1988). *Historical, Political and Technical Development of ARABSAT*. Unpublished doctoral disseration, Northwestern University, Evanston, Illinois.

-- Agee, Warren K., Phillip H. Ault, and Edwin Emery (1988). *Introduction to Mass Communication*, New York: Harper & Row Publishers.

-- Al-Saadon, H. T. (1990). *The Role of ARABSAT in Television Program Exchange in the Arab World*. Unpublished doctoral disseration, The Ohio State University, Columbus, Ohio.

-- Alter, Jonathan (1990). "Ted's Global Village," *Newsweek*, June 11, 48-52.

-- Alter, Jonathan (1991). "When CNN Hit Its Target," *Newsweek* January 20, 41.

-- Amer, F. Y. (1990). Facsimile from ARABSAT. Interview, Chairman of the Engineering Sector, Egyptian Ministry of Information Files, Cairo, Egypt.

-- Amin, Hussein Y. "Arianespace Issues Launch Manifest" (1990). *PR Newswire*, May 15.

-- Amin, H. Y. and M. Murrie (1992). "Development and Impact of the Egyptian International Television Network." Paper presented at the International Association for Mass Communication Research, Guaruja, Brazil.

-- ------- (1990). "Egyptian Photographic Industry... Can It Solve Its Problems?" *Business Monthly*, Sept. 6 (8), 34-40.

-- Anderson, Robin (1991). "The Press, the Public, and the New World Order: The Media Coverage of the Gulf War," *Media Development* October (Special), 20-26.

-- Attia, Ibrahim (1990). Engineer, Head of Propagation Department, ERTU, Egyptian Ministry of Information Files, Cairo, Egypt.

-- Basyouni, Amin (1989). Vice-President of ERTU, Egyptian Ministry of Information Files, Cairo, Egypt.

-- Bertrand, Claude-Jean (1989). "American Cultural Imperialism: A Myth?" In Michael C. Emery and Ted C. Smythe, eds., *Readings in Mass Communication*. Dubuque, Iowa: Wm. C. Brown, 259-272.

-- Blackwood, Roy (1983). "The Content of News Photos: Roles Portrayed by Men and Women," *Journalism Quarterly* (60), Winter, 211.

-- Boyd, D. (1982). *Broadcasting in the Arab World*. Philadelphia: Temple University Press.

-- Broad, W. J. (1985). "Shuttle Lofts Satellites for Arab Lands and P.L.O." *New York Times*. October 16, 25.

-- "CNN's Global Village" (1990). *Newsweek*, June 18, 46-50.

-- "CNN's Place in History" (1991). *Broadcasting*, March 4, 29.

-- "Cross-Fromtier Bradcasting" (1992). The Economist , May 2, 21-22,28.

-- Dabbous, Sonia (1982). *The Political Impact on Egypt's Press: A Comparative Study of the Press Before and After the 1952 Revolution, 1923-1970*. Ph.D. dissertation, University of Kent.

-- ------- (1985). "The Role of the Press in Egypt's Democratic Experience." Paper presented at the Annual Meeting of the Middle East Studies Association, New Orleans, Louisiana.

-- Davidian, Geoff (1991). "Press Told it Sleights Friendly Islamic Side," *Houston Chronicle*, Jan. 26, 3.

-- Dilawari, Sudesh Rani, Robert Stewart and Don Flournoy (1991). "Development News on CNN World Report," *Gazette*, March (47), 121-137.

-- DTVB Leasing Contract (1990). Egyptian Ministry of Information Files, Cairo, Egypt.

-- Egypt Country Report (1989-90). London: The Economist Intelligence Unit.

-- Egypt Country Report (1991-92). London: The Economist Intelligence Unit.

-- El-Desoukry, Morad Ibrahim (1992). "The American Mass Media Maneuver During the Gulf War," *The Arab Mass Communication Studies*, 68 (July-September), published by the Arab Center for Communication Studies.

-- El-Tarabichi, Maha (1975). *A Content Analysis of Cartoons in Al-Ahram Before and After the Lifting of Press Censorship*. Master's thesis, The American University in Cairo, Dept. of Journalism and Mass Communication.

-- Fahmy, Rania (1990). "Direct Broadcasting, But is it Welcome?" *Business Monthly*, September 6 (8), 23-28.

-- Fayoumi, A. (1990). Head Transmission Project Department, ERTU. (Egyptian Ministry of Information Files, Cairo, Egypt).

-- ------- (1991, May). French to launch ARABSAT 3. (Egyptian Ministry of Information Files, Cairo, Egypt).

-- ------- (1990). Head Transmission Project Department, ERTU. (Egyptian Ministry of Information Files, Cairo, Egypt)

-- Fisk, Robert (1992). "Challenging the Might of the Sound-Bite," *The Independent*, (Jan. 8), 13.

-- Fitzgerald, Mark (1990)."'Development' Journalism Dying Along with NWICO," *Editor & Publisher*, (May 26), 49.

-- Fore, William F. (1991). "The Shadow War in the Gulf," *Media Development*, October (Special), 51-52.

-- Fouad, Marwan (1991). "Cairo Thinks Again," *The Middle East* (July), 23-24.

-- Fouhy, Ed (1991). "Huffing and Puffing: Wounded Reputation in the Desert," *Communicator*, (April), 17-19.

-- Franklin, Stephen (1991). "The Kingdom and Its Messengers," *Columbia Journalism Review* (July/August), 24-27.

-- Galtung, Johan (1979). "A Structural Theory of Imperialism." in George Modelski, ed., *Transnational Corporations and World Order*. New York. W.H. Freeman, 155-172.

-- Ghareeb, Edmund (ed.) (1983). *Split Vision: The Portrayal of Arabs in the American Media*, Washington, D.C.: American Arab Affairs Council.

-- Grcic-Polic, Jelena (1989). "Communication and Development: An Historical Overview," in Biserka Cvjeticanin, ed., *Communications for Development*. Zagreb: Institute for Developing Countries, 7-37.

-- Hafez, Salah El-Din (1991). *Information Crisis During the Gulf Crisis*, Cairo: Arabic Center for Communication Studies.

-- Haga, Mostafa (1991). "How Egyptian Mass Media Managed the Gulf Crisis" (Arabic), in Hafez (1991).

-- Haggag, M. (1991). "Keif Wagah El Ealam Al Masri Azmet El Khaleg," *Drasat Islamia* (64), 108-115.

-- Haynes, Robert D. Jr. (1984). "Test of Galtung's Theory of Structural Imperialism," in Robert L. Stevenson and Donald Lewis Shaw, eds., *Foreign News and the New World Information Order*. Ames: The Iowa State University Press.

-- Hedges, Chris (1991). "The Unilaterals," *Columbia Journalism Review* (July/August), 27-29.

-- Henry, William A., III (1992). "History As It Happens," *Time*, January 6, 14-17.

-- "How the Egyptian Mass Media Administered the Gulf Crisis" (1991). A study by the Egyptian Radio and Television Union to document the mass media's work during the Gulf War. Arab Republic of Egypt (May).

-- Hussein, Mustafa (1990). *The Intimidating Marshall*, (Arabic) Cairo: Al Zahara.

-- Ibrahim, Youssef M. (1992). "TV Is Beamed at Arabs. The Arabs Beam Back." *The New York Times*, March 4.

-- Ivacic, Pero (1989). "The Pool of News Agencies of Non-Aligned Countries," in Biserka Cvjeticanin, ed., *Communications for Development*. Zagreb: Institute for Developing Countries, 121-140.

--"Journalists Condemn Wartime Censorship" (1991), *Broadcasting*, Sept. 21, 28.

-- Katz, Elihu (1992). "The End of Journalism,: Notes on Watching the War," *Journal of Communication* 42 (3), 5-13.

-- Khalil, A. (1990). Head of SpaceNet. Egyptian Ministry of Information Files, Cairo, Egypt.

-- Khalil, Nevine (1991). "Cartoon Strips in the Egyptian Press During the Gulf

Crisis," unpublished research report, the American University in Cairo, Dept. of Journalism and Mass Communication.

-- Kobre, Kenneth (1980). *Photojournalism: The Professional's Approach*, Stoneham, Mass.: Butterworth Publishers.

-- Koeppel, Barbara (1988). *The Press in the Middle East: Constraint, Consensus, Censorship*. Washington, D.C.: Middle East Research & Information Project.

-- LaMay, Craig, Martha FitzSimon and Jeanne Sahadi (eds.) (1991). *The Media at War: The Press and the Persian Gulf Crisis*. New York: Gannett Foundation Media Center at Columbia University.

-- Larson, Ernest (1991). "Gulf War TV," *Jump Cut* (36), 3-10.

-- Leibes, Tamar (1992). "Comparing *Intifadeh* and the Gulf War on U.S. and Israeli Television," *Critical Studies in Mass Communication* 9 (1) 44-55.

-- Leo, John (1991). "Lessons from a Sanitized War," *U.S. News and World Report*, March 18, 26.

-- Lesch, Ann Mosely (1991). "Contrasting Reaction to the Persian Gulf Crisis: Egypt, Syria, Jordan, and the Palestinians," *Middle East Journal* 43 (1), 30-50.

-- Lester, Paul and Ron Smith (1990) "African-American Photo Coverage in Life, Newsweek, and Time, 1937-1988," *Journalism Quarterly* (67), Spring, 128-136.

-- MacBride, Sean, et al. (1980). *Many Voices, One World*. Paris, London and New York: UNESCO.

-- Malik, Rex (1991). "The Media's Gulf War: Notes and Issues," *Intermedia*, March-April (19, 2), 4-7.

-- Marsot, Afaf Lutifi Al-Sayyid (1971). "The Cartoon in Egypt," *Comparative Studies in Society and History*, 13 (1), 2-15.

-- Masmoudi, Mustapha (1978). *The New World Information Order*. Document No. 34, submitted to the UNESCO International Commission for the Study of Communication Problems.

-- Meyer, William H. (1991). "Structure of North-South Informational Flows: An Empirical Test of Galtung's Theory," *Journalism Quarterly* (68), (1-2), 230-237.

-- Miller, Susan (1975). "The Content of News Photos," *Journalism Quarterly* 52:72, Spring, 338-339.

-- Mishinski, Judy (1990). "Live from Planet Earth," *Cairo Today*, September, 51-56.

-- Mohamed, Azza A. and Solafa A. Goueli (1992). "CNN in Egypt: A Critique," unpublished research report, the American University in Cairo, Dept. of Journalism and Mass Communication.

-- Nain, Zahromon (1991). "The Malaysian Press: Ethnicising the Issue?" *Media Development* October (Special), 30-31.

-- Napoli, James J. (1991). "Development Journalism: The Press and the Nation Travel the Same Road," *Journalism Quarterly of the Dept. of Mass Communication* (X, 7-8), 25-33. University of the Punjab: Lahore, Pakistan.

-- ----- (1992). "Egyptian Sleight of Hand," *Index on Censorship* 2: 21-23.

-- Nasser, Munir (1982). *Press Control Around the World*. New York: Praeger Publishers.

-- *News and the New World Order: A Report* (1991). Gannett Foundation Media Center, New York.

-- O'Heffernan, Patrick (1991). "Television and the Security of Nations: Learning from the Gulf War," *Television Quarterly* (1), 5-13.

-- "Press Group Launches Campaign to 'Pull Plug' on CNN's Arnett" (1991), *Broadcasting*, February 18, 61.

-- Revzin, Philip, Peter Waldman and Peter Gumbel (1990). "Ted Turner's CNN Gains Influence and 'Diplomatic Role,'" *Wall Street Journal*, February 1.

-- Rugh, William (1979). *The Arab Press*. New York: Syracuse University.

-- Salama, Salama Ahmed (1991). "Foreign Networks" (Arabic), *Al-Ahram*, June 2, 6.

-- Samir, Abeer (1991). "CNN in Egypt," unpublished research report, the American University in Cairo, Dept. of Journalism and Mass Communication.

-- Schiller, Herbert I. (1971). *Mass Communications and American Empire*. Boston: Beacon Press.

-- Schuneman, R. Smith (1972). *Photographic Communication*, New York: Hastings House.

-- Seberny, Muhammadi (1984), "The 'World of News' Study -- Results of Cooperation," *Journal of Communication*, Winter.

-- Smith, Anthony (1990). "Media Globalism in the Age of Consumer Sovereignty," *Gannett Center Journal*, Fall, 1-20.

-- Smith, Vern E. (1990). "The Whole World is Watching," *Sunday Times Magazine*, October 7.

-- Schleifer, S. Abdullah (1991). "WMNS Situation Report," Feb. 1 (Internal Document, Jeddah).

-- Shadroui, George (1991). "WMNS Offers Pro-Alliance Perspective on War,"

Middle East Times, February 19, 3.

-- Traber, Michael and Philip Lee (eds.) (1991). "After the Gulf War: New Communication Problems to Solve," *Media Development*, October (Special), 1.

-- Tschirgi, Dan and Bassam Tibi (1991). "Perspectives on the Gulf Crisis," *Cairo Papers in Social Science* (14,1), Spring.

-- Tunstall, Jeremy (1977). *The Media Are American*. New York: Columbia University Press.

-- Turkistani, A. S. (1990). *News Exchange via ARABSAT and News Values of Arab Television News People*. Unpublished doctoral dissertation, Indiana University.

-- Turner, Ted (1991). "The Gulf War and Media Censorship," Speech given at the Ted Turner Symposium on Media and Social Responsibilities, Montana State University sponsorship, Big Sky, Montana.

-- "US, China Begin Talks to Review 1989 Satellite Launch Agreement," (1990) *BNA International Trade Daily*, July 11,

-- Vatikiotis, P.J. (1991). *The History of Modern Egypt from Muhammad Ali to Mubarak*. London: Weidenfeld and Nicolson.

-- Vincent, Richard (1991). "The Role of Elites in News Originization and News Manipulation," paper presented at Istanbul, Turkey: International Association for Mass Communication Research.

-- Vitray, Laura, John Mills, and Roscoe Ellard (1939). *Pictorial Journalism*, New York: McGraw-Hill.

-- Webster, Richard (1990). *A Brief History of Blasphemy*. London: Orwell Press.

-- Weisenborn, Ray (1979). "Egyptian English Press Dependence on International Wire Services," paper presented at the Oregon Center for Graduate Study, Portland: NSF Regional Conference.

-- ------- (1990). "Cultural Imperialism or Balanced News Flow? Cases of Egypt and Korea," paper presented at California State University-Fullerton: Conference on International/Intercultural Communication.

-- Woodburn, Bert (1947). "Reader Interest in Newspaper Pictures," *Journalism Quarterly* (24) Autumn, 197.

-- Zuckerman, Lawrence (1988). "The Global Village Tunes In," *Time*, June 6, 77.

CONTRIBUTORS

CONTRIBUTORS

Hussein Amin (Ph.D., Ohio State) is a consultant to various media organizations, including the Egyptian Radio and Television Union. He is an Assistant Professor of Journalism and Mass Communication at the American University in Cairo.

Magda Bagneid (Ph.D., Cairo University) has a weekly radio program, "Stars on Egyptian Land," does free lance reporting, and teaches mass communication at the American University in Cairo.

Richard Boylan (Ph.D., University of Iowa) is actively engaged in photo documentation research and is an Associate Professor of Journalism and Mass Communication, the American University in Cairo.

Sonia Dabbous (Ph.D., University of Kent) is the Foreign Affairs Editor for *Akhbar El-Youm* and teaches Arabic press history at the American University in Cairo.

Dina Lamey (M.A., American University in Cairo) is currently teaching in Saudi Arabia.

James Napoli (M.A., Boston College) is a career journalist who has worked on numerous U.S. newspapers. He has extensively researched the Egyptian press and currently is Chair of Journalism and Mass Communication at the American University in Cairo.

S.A. Schleifer (M.A., American University of Beirut) has been a journalist, including NBC Bureau Chief, covering the Middle East for 25 years. He covered the Gulf crisis from Saudi Arabia. He is the Director, Kamal Adham Center for Television Journalism at the American University in Cairo's Department of Journalism and Mass Communication.

Ted Turner is the owner of several broadcast networks, including CNN. He serves on the Board of Trustees for the Adham Center for Television Journalism at the American University in Cairo.

John Tusa (1st Degree, Trinity College, Cambridge) is Managing Director of the British Broadcasting Corporation's World Service. A journalist who has held foreign assignments in the Soviet Union and China, he received the

Royal Television Society's Journalist of the Year Award in 1983. His most recent book is, *A World in Your Ear*, published in 1992.

Ray Weisenborn (Ph.D., Michigan State) has been a Senior Fulbright Fellow and broadcast journalist in Europe and Asia. He co-developed the Ted Turner Symposium on Media and Social Responsibilities sponsored by Montana State University. Currently he is a Professor of Journalism and Mass Communication at the American University in Cairo.